A Book of Magical Powders & Oils

Bree NicGarran

Foreword by
Lauren Goodnight

Pestlework: A Book of Magical Powders & Oils is © 2017 by Bree NicGarran. Some of the material used was previously published in The Witches' Cupboard © 2015 by Anna Zollinger and Bree NicGarran, and Grovedaughter Witchery: Practical Spellcraft © 2017 by Bree NicGarran. All material is intellectual property of Bree NicGarran and does not infringe upon the copyright of previous publications. Any resemblance to works or recipes created by other authors or practitioners is purely coincidental.

This book is distributed in Paperback and Electronic format with DSRM enabled. All rights to this book and its' contents are reserved, including the right to reproduce the book or portions thereof in any format. No part of this book may be used or reproduced in any manner, including internet publication, without written consent from the author, except in the case of brief quotations embodied in critical articles or reviews, or in other manners, formats, and lengths congruent with Fair Use.

The author does not endorse third-party transactions outside of the designated sale channels, nor do they have any authority or responsibility concerning the unaffiliated third party resale of this material, or private party transactions between other members of the public. The author shall not be held liable for the resale or redistribution outside of the designated sale channels. Those companies designated as the appropriate sale channels shall hold all responsibility for any problems with the book and/or its' delivery.

Any references or sources contained within this work are current at the time of publication. The author cannot guarantee that these references or their locations and availability will continue to be maintained after publication. All external products or materials in this book are the property or and registered trademarks, products, etc. of the companies that produce them. The author makes no attempt to claim ownership or copyright over these products.

The author considers the practical safety warnings contained herein to be sufficient to discourage the illegal, harmful, or immoral use of the materials. Any irresponsible, dangerous, harmful; or otherwise unsafe or illegal use of the recipes and methods contained herein (or byproducts thereof) is the fault and responsibility of the reader themselves. The author shall not be held liable or responsible for such usage.

If you have purchased or received a copy of this book which reads PROOF on any area of it, you have obtained a limited supply early release copy. The content of such a copy may differ from the final published edition. If you have received a redistributed copy of this book without a cover, or in an illegal electronic format that is not congruent with the formats distributed through parties designated for sale via the author: You should be aware that such a copy is likely stolen property and the author has not been fairly compensated for her work. Please refrain from distributing or receiving such illegal copies, as the author is not under contract with any publishing house and only receives royalties from direct, legal sales.

If you enjoyed this book,
please consider leaving a review
on Amazon.com or Goodreads.com.

Want to see this book in your local pagan shop?
The author can be reached for business inquiries at
BreeNicGarran@outlook.com.

Wordpress: http://BreeNicGarran.wordpress.com
Tumblr: http://BreeNicGarran.tumblr.com

Table of Contents

Acknowledgements
Author's Note
Foreword: Lauren Goodnight

Introduction
Preparation and Use of Magical Powders
Preparation and Use of Magical Oils
Safety Tips

Section One: Magical Powders
All-Purpose Blessing Powder
All-Purpose Cursing Powder
All-Purpose Warding Powder
Attraction Powder
Beauty Salt
Binding Powder
Blocking Salt
Bree's Banishing Powder
Bree's Black Salt Blend
Bree's Luck Salt
Business Blessing Powder
Casting Salt
Catalyst Spice Powder
Clean House Powder
Come Hither Powder
Cover My Tracks Powder
Curseturner Powder
Dead Man's Dust
Deflection Salt
Done Deal Powder
Dream Dust
"Eye of Sauron" Revelation Powder
Find-A-Friend Powder
Get Thee Hence Powder
Ghost-Be-Gone Powder
Harmony Salt
Heal Thy Body Powder
Heal Thy Heart Powder
Health and Wealth Powder
Hexbreaker Powder

Hold Strong Powder
Home Blessing Powder
Honest Passion Powder
Instant Glamour Powder
Inspiration Salt
Inversion Powder
Invisibility Powder
Jackpot Powder
Jar of Dirt Protection Power
Jinx Salt
Jobfinder Powders
Lion's Roar Powder
Long Haul Powder
Love-Me Powder
Lover-Be-True Powder
Nightmare Dust
Notice-Me Powder
Obfuscation Powder
Outta My Way Powder
Paper Tiger Powder
Peacekeeper Powder
Persuasion Powder
Pet Protection Powder
Pixie Dust
Promisekeeper Powder
Prosperity Salt
Protection Powder
Purification Salt
Quick Draw Powder
Rest In Peace Powder
Rose Salt
Sealing Salt
Show-Me Salt
Sickroom Salt
Spirit Salt
Star Power Powder
STFU Powder
Sweetening Powder
Threshold Powder
Traveler's Luck Powder
Turning Salt
Weather Magic Powders

Section Two: Magical Oils
Attraction, Love, & Glamour
Augmentation
Catalysts & Change
Cleansing & Banishing
Divination & Spirit Work
Healing & Restoration
Hexing & Hexbreaking
Luck, Money, & Success
Persuasion & Manipulation
Protection & Blessing
Miscellaneous

Sample Recipe Sheets

Online Resources

Bibliography & Recommended Reading

About the Author

Related Works

Acknowledgements

First and foremost, I would like to thank Anna Zollinger (Boyett), my co-author from *The Sisters Grimmoire* and *The Witches' Cupboard*. Her advice and support were instrumental in helping me get my start as a published writer, and I wish her all the best in her future projects, whatever they may be.

I'd like to thank the online pagan community, particularly the denizens of Tumblr who have found their way to my blog. Their enthusiasm has buoyed me through some difficult times, and I am grateful for the honest feedback that they've given me on all of my projects thus far.

My heartfelt gratitude goes out to my long-time beta readers and superhero-grade helpers, Lauren and Rebecca, ready as ever to correct my grammar, point out typos, and occasionally remind me that even writers need to sleep. I also wish to thank Deb Foley, owner and proprietor of Mystic Moon in Norfolk, VA, for her support and encouragement, and for giving my books their first spot in a brick-and-mortar store.

As always, I want to thank my husband, who has always supported my dreams and my drive, and is eternally proud of me, even when I have a hard time being proud of myself.

Lastly, I thank my most loyal supporters, my midnight study buddies, my furry little helpers, Havoc and Penny. Best familiars a witch could ask for.

Author's Note

The views expressed in this book are the personal opinions, advice, and experiences of the author. They are not intended to be taken as absolute truth, nor are they intended to invalidate the religious, spiritual, or moral views of the reader. They are meant only as a suggestion and are limited by the knowledge of the author.

The recipes and spells in this book are the original creations of the author, as used in her personal practice, which specializes in charms, powders, and preventative magics. Any similarity to the workings of other practitioners is purely coincidental.

It should be noted that the author lives in Eastern North America and hence, the availability of certain substances, or the designation of a substance as "commonly available," is entirely based on that geographic location. Your regional availability may vary.

No spell or charm in this book is intended to replace mundane safety measures or medical or psychiatric treatment of any kind. Please exercise caution and consult your doctor before trying alternative treatment or stopping any current treatment.

Magic is not a substitute for practical action. It can only augment what you choose to do.

Please always be sure to double-check your sources, refer to practical texts, and think critically before using any information in your own practice.

Foreword

When I was nineteen, I went into my very first witchy shop. Candles, crystals, incense, cards, jewelry...it was overwhelming in a way. I remember what I bought that day too, and this is the important bit: One book on magical herbs, five packets of herbs/resins (verbena, dragon's blood, white sage, frankincense, myrrh) and a mortar and pestle. I didn't know why, but when I looked at that marble bowl, at the simple curve of the grinding stone, I knew *this* was a witch's tool.

I brought it home and promptly ruined it with resin.

I never said I had common sense.

But with that little incident, I learned to grab a book on a subject and work from there. I didn't ruin my next magical tool, nor the one after. Guidance is often difficult to find in solitary practice and I personally turned even more towards books and later the internet. Sadly, most of what I found wasn't aligned with my beliefs, even if there were useful parts in there somewhere.

What I never saw was a simple powder spellbook with intuition, common sense, and no religious agenda. Then I watched Pestlework come into being and breathed easy. I've known Bree for years and I admired her dedication to the craft and to her writing, but it was her dedication to the secular basics that I grew to admire most. Pestlework started when Bree decided to move from the basics (please do look for her work, Grovedaughter Witchery, to see for yourself what I mean) into teaching one of her specialties, crafting oils and powders. It was kind of amazing to watch her excitement for this project carry through months of toil, and in your hands you hold the product.

Grab your bowl and stick, your mortar and pestle, and march bravely forward with this guidance...but perhaps don't ruin your first set!

Go forth with intent,

Lauren Goodnight

Introduction

Preparation & Use of Magical Powders

Suggested Materials:

- Mortar & Pestle (or Spice Grinder)
- Funnel (must fit inside mouth of storage container)
- Mesh Strainer (must fit inside rim of funnel)
- Storage Container with Tight-fitting Lid

To make herb powders, grind each ingredient separately to produce fine powder. Sieve the material through a mesh strainer into a collection dish or directly into the storage jar; this removes the larger leftover pieces and gives you cleaner powdered herb. Putting a funnel under the mesh strainer reduces lost material and makes collection much easier.

When you're ready to make your magical powder, combine the component powders in a collection dish in their respective quantities, mix well, and bottle immediately. You can also combine the components directly in a new storage jar, then put the lid on and swirl or shake gently to blend them. If you're going to shake the jar, just make sure that the lid is on tightly.

I highly recommend glass or sturdy plastic jars with screw-top lids for storing your powders. Cork-top jars and bottles where the cork is easily removed are not secure and will spill everywhere if tipped. Food storage containers, even with tight-fitting lids, do not always fully contain powdered material unless you're very careful. Plastic sandwich baggies or jewelry baggies are also useful for storing powders, so long as they are clearly labeled and kept away from anything that much puncture or tear them.

When creating your own magical powder recipes, it's wise to go slightly heavier on the less expensive or more readily-available components. Examples of this can be seen in the pages of this book, as it is generally easier for me to rely on spice aisle seasonings or the lower-priced powdered herbs from botanical sellers when concocting my own formulas.

Substances like Salt, Black Pepper, Basil, Rosemary, Green Sage, Thyme, Crushed Peppers, Rose Petals, and certain woods like Cedar may be cheaply obtained from mundane sources and make good basic ingredients for magical powders. When in doubt, or when running low on a component, you can always consult a list of magical plant correspondences and choose a substance with the same magical purpose which is more affordable or more readily available.

The nice thing about making magical powders is that once you've got a jar of something ready, it's very easy to toss a pinch or two where it'll do the most good, even on your busiest days or when your energy is low.

Case in point - House-cleansing needed on a day when you have no energy to spare for gathering jars and blending herbs? No problem! Toss some dried sage or cedar chips into a burning bowl, light it up, and add a few pinches of Clean House Powder along with your intent. Easy peasy. Granted, there's some effort involved in making the powder in the first place, but it can save you a lot of time and energy later on.

Helpful Hints

If you choose to use a mortar and pestle to grind your herbs, I recommend getting a larger one, at least 2-3" deep, with a heavy pestle. Stone is the ideal material, as you'll need the solidity and the weight, and the rougher texture of the inside of the mortar in order to grind herbs effectively. Wooden or metal mortar and pestle sets don't work as well, especially for barks and roots. The smoother texture and lighter pestle weight don't give you the same result as stone, and they take much more time and effort to be effective.

Marble is my material of choice for M&P sets, with granite running a very close second. Both of these are fairly standard. A goodly number of the stone M&P sets you'll find on witchcraft supply sites are marble or granite and will be marked as such. Look for photos of the inside of the mortar bowl with any online listing; make sure that there is a nice rough texture for the plant material to be worked against. As previously mentioned, a smooth surface is not much good for what you're trying to accomplish.

Many M&P sets you'll find for kitchen or pharmaceutical use are ceramic. These tend to be the most affordable and are useful when you're first getting started, but they share the problems of smooth mortar bowls and light pestle weight. Ceramic sets also tend to be on the small and shallow side. I keep a medium-sized ceramic M&P for grinding eggshells, but I would not recommend it for anything hardier than that.

Heavy-duty lava stone M&Ps are available from some kitchen supply stores. These are great for both texture and weight, and easily crush down even the toughest barks and resins. However, the porous texture of the lava stone means that the desired powder sometimes gets trapped in the surface of the bowl and is not easily cleaned or retrieved. Also, before use, the mortar requires a very thorough scrub with water and dry rice to remove loose stone particles.

If you are working with large chunks of wood or resin that need to be broken down into manageable chunks before being worked with a spice grinder or smaller M&P set, a lava stone M&P may be helpful. Just make sure that you get one of good quality, which may mean shelling out a fair amount of money. You'll also need a safe place to store it; these sets are very heavy and will cause injury if they fall on unsuspecting heads or feet.

Speaking of resins, if you're going to be using your stone M&P to grind them, make sure that you brush some cornstarch onto the inside of the mortar bowl before you begin. Incense resins like Copal, Myrrh, Frankincense, and Dragon's Blood are composed of hardened sticky tree sap. As such, they become tacky when broken down and tend to adhere to and stain the mortar. This is a very quick way to ruin a good M&P set, as the resulting residue is very difficult, if not impossible, to remove. A light coating of cornstarch helps to keep the resin from sticking, gives you more powdered resin to work with, and saves your beloved M&P from becoming a non-functioning curio piece. (I have found that dusting-sized amounts of cornstarch do not noticeably affect the quality of the resulting powder.)

Mortar and pestle sets do take a fair amount of elbow grease, and even with several minutes of hard work, they may not grind the plant material completely to powder. Using a mesh strainer and a funnel can help to separate the useable powder from the leftover plant pieces. These can still be used for other spells or loose incense, so don't throw them out if you don't have to. Remember, witchlings - waste not, want not.

For folks who don't have the time or the ability to labor over a stone bowl for ages to make herb powders, an electric coffee bean grinder can be a witch's best friend. Hamilton Beach makes a decent one that retails for under $30.00 (USD) and works extremely well for small batches of most plants, even barks and roots. It's suitable for occasional personal use, and I've been happy with mine for several years. For frequent, high-volume, or heavy-duty grinding, you may want something larger. Make sure you comparison-shop online or at your local kitchen supply store before making a purchase

Whichever model you choose, you'll need to let it rest for few minutes between batches and clean it out with dry paper towels and a brush after each use. Never, ever use water on the inside of electronic spice grinders or you'll risk shorting out the motor and it will stop working. If you don't clean it out, or forget to let it rest between grindings, the motor can burn out, so be careful.

Standard manual spice grinders for things like nutmeg can also be useful. These tend to be small and mostly useful for plant material. I would suggest leaving the grinding of tough roots and barks to a heavy M&P or a particularly stalwart electric spice grinder.

Powdered versions of some herbs are also available in grocery stores or through online botanical merchants. I have included my favorite suppliers on the Online Resources page. Some merchants will sell small amounts of herbs, others only sell in bulk. Use your best judgment according to how much powder your personal craft requires. A little bit of powdered herb goes a long way, after all!

When shopping around for herb powders, particularly online, I highly recommend looking for herbs from food or botanical sellers before most pagan shops. Powdered herbs are difficult to identify, and there's no way of telling from a website listing whether the substance has been augmented with cheaper herbs for bulk. Plants and spices meant for the culinary or botanical industries have to pass purity and safety standards at some point during their production, and therefore you are just about guaranteed that what you're buying matches what's on the label. This is part of the reason that I recommend spice-aisle herbs for witches who are just getting their start; if the bottle says Lemongrass, you can be pretty darned sure that you're getting Lemongrass, rather than Lemongrass-and-something-cheaper-that-looks-enough-like-Lemongrass-that-no-one-will-notice.

And speaking of grass, make sure that you don't use any powder containing salt on your lawn, your garden, or anywhere that it might fall on bare earth or living plants. Salt poses a significant threat to vegetation and soil quality and can permanently alter the ground on which it falls if it is present in sufficient quantities. There is a reason that we hear of ancient soldiers "salting the ground behind them" in order to destroy the lands of their enemies. Once a field is salted, you'll need more than magic to get anything to grow there again.

Several of the recipes in this book mention the use of Black Sugar. Despite what some folks seem to think, this is not a rare mystical substance. Black sugar may be obtained from some shops that sell baking decorations, particularly around the Halloween season. If it is not available in your area, regular white sugar mixed with charcoal may be substituted.

There are suggested uses included with all of the powder recipes in this book, but the lists on each entry are far from comprehensive. There are dozens of ways to use magical powders in your witchcraft, and I encourage you, dear reader, to experiment and find out which methods work best for you.

On a final note, the magical powders and oils in this book are not to be ingested, inhaled, or used for topical ailments, save for the occasional light dusting of hands or feet. They are not to be thrown at other people, blown into another person's face, or put into their food or drink. If any adverse or allergic reaction occurs, discontinue use of the powder immediately. All this should go without saying, and I'll repeat myself in the Safety Instructions, but for the sake of thoroughness, I feel the need to include a reminder here.

Preparation and Use of Magical Oils

Suggested Materials:

- Carrier Oil (ex. Almond, Sunflower, Olive, etc.)
- Herb Blend or Essential Oils
- Glass Jar
- Funnel
- Coffee Filter
- Storage Container with Tight-fitting Lid
- Label

To make your own magical oils, start with a bland carrier oil, such as those listed above. A bland oil will more readily absorb the fragrance of the herbs with which it is infused. Select fresh or dried herbs that will suit your purposes. If you wish, you can also use essential oils in addition to or in place of the herbs.

In a glass jar, combine 1 part herb blend with 2 parts oil. Leave about an inch of air at the top to allow room for shaking. Cap the jar tightly, label it with the contents and date, and leave it in a warm dry place or a sunny windowsill to steep for no less than two weeks. Shake the jar daily to help the infusion process along.

If you want to use a faster method, you can also simmer the oil and herbs in a small saucepan on very low heat for about one to two hours, stirring occasionally. This method may work better than jar infusion if you plan to use fresh ingredients as opposed to dried ones. Some herbalists also recommend a double-boiler method using an open saucepan filled one-third with water and a glass jar containing the herbs and oil, but this method takes a great deal of practice and may be problematic for beginners.

When it is finished, strain the oil through a coffee filter into a bottle for storage. Use a funnel to prevent spills. Seal and label the bottle with a name, purpose, and date. This may seem excessive, but trust me when I say that you will not remember which bottle is which when you need them without clear labeling and differentiation. (It's happened to me. Mistook a vial of Hot Foot Banishing Oil for the much less caustic Brim With Vim Vitality Oil once. Would not recommend the experience.)

Magical oils may be added to any spell where their purpose is appropriate. They can also be additives in floor washes and room sprays. Some witches also use them in bath magic, which I only recommend doing if you know for certain that you are not allergic or sensitive to any of the oil's ingredients. In general, I don't recommend magical oils for internal use, purely for safety reasons, and topically only with great caution.

In some cases, fresh ingredients for your blend may yield a stronger scent than their dried equivalents. These items, in my experience, give a better quality of scent and magical efficacy if used when fresh for making oils.

Some examples include the following:

- Certain Aromatic Herbs (basil, rosemary, sage)
- Mints (peppermint, spearmint, catnip, etc)
- Peppers (any sort, but mostly chilies)
- Citrus Peels (orange, lemon, lime, etc)
- Horseradish Root (sliced or grated)
- Ginger Root (sliced or grated)
- Lemongrass (sliced or minced)
- Rose Petals (any color, roughly chopped)

It's important to note that oils made with fresh ingredients may not last as long and have a higher chance of developing mold or turning rancid because of the water content of non-dried ingredients. If you choose to use fresh herbs, you may want to cover the mouth of the jar with cheesecloth or a paper towel during steeping to let the water evaporate. The less water in the mix, the less likely it is that your oil will turn moldy or rancid. If you choose to use a porous covering for your jar, be extra careful when shaking or swirling the oil so that it doesn't slop out and make a mess.

Roots and peels should be sliced or grated for best effect. Aromatic herbs and flowers should be roughly chopped or cut and sifted as your space needs dictate. Peppers, whether fresh or dried, are almost a class unto themselves, and you can use them whole or slice them depending on just how potent you want your oil to be.

I always recommend a little extra caution when working with capsicum (the substance that makes peppers spicy) since it's an irritant and will cause an awful burning sensation if it makes contact with pretty much anything in the facial region. Wash your hands thoroughly with degreasing soap and water after handling peppers to decrease this risk.

In general, dried ingredients should be your default for infusing magical oils, especially if you're just starting to experiment with the process of making them at home. Dried herbs are generally cheaper, easier to use, and won't go bad if you don't use them right away.

Essential oils are good additives as well, and can be used in addition to or in place of herbal ingredients if you like. Exercise the same caution with essential oils that you would with the herbs themselves as far as health risks and allergies go. Also note that essential oils should *never* be applied directly to the skin without a carrier oil to dilute them.

When creating your own recipes, you can have as many or as few ingredients as you like. I usually keep mine to three or four for the sake of simplicity. Your methods may vary on this point; you can use as many as you feel is necessary, but more ingredients may muddle the mix and result in odd scents. I suggest experimenting with small amounts of oil and herbs before making larger batches, so you have some idea of what you're getting before you go wasting a bunch of supplies on something that turns out horrible.

And remember, don't beat yourself up if you don't get it right the first time. This is chemistry as well as cooking, and it may take time and a bit of trial and error to hit your stride and find the combinations that work best for you. Practice makes perfect!

Safety Tips

As a general rule, the magical powders and oils in this book are *not* to be ingested, inhaled, or used for topical ailments, save for the occasional light dusting of hands or feet. They are not to be thrown at other people, blown into another person's face, or put into their food or drink. If any adverse or allergic reaction occurs, discontinue use of the substance immediately.

Yes, I know I'm repeating myself, and I'll probably do so again later in the text, but this is very important. I cannot control what is done with the information I provide in these pages, but I *can* make every effort to ensure that I've made myself clear on the inclusion of safety information and instructions for proper use of these substances, and hope that my readers will exercise decency and common sense in the use of the material.

Be aware that some of the substances listed as ingredients for the following recipes are harmful if ingested. Others should be avoided by those who are pregnant, nursing, or looking to have a child. All powders and oils should be kept well out of the reach of children and pets to prevent accidental inhalation or ingestion. Should accidental contact or ingestion occur, thoroughly cleanse the affected area as much as you are able and contact a physician or a veterinarian right away.

Throughout this book, substances which are dangerous if ingested or inhaled are marked with a single asterisk (*). Substances which should be avoided by those who are pregnant or nursing are marked with a double asterisk (**). If you are on medication or have chronic health issues, consult a physician before you begin mucking about with powders and oils, in case of potentially dangerous interactions.

Do not physically dose others with magical powders or oils (or indeed any substance) without their knowledge and consent. None of the substances within these pages are meant to be taken internally and may cause an adverse reaction if ingested. Do not put any powder or oil listed in this book into someone's food or drink. Do not throw it at people or blow it in their faces. This is *assault* and aside from it being a rotten thing to do, you could get in a great deal of trouble, especially if the person in question becomes ill. There are very goods reasons that the methods of use you will find listed in this book largely deal with sympathetic or similarly indirect methods of application.

On the heels of that, do not dose animals with magical powders or oils for any reason. None of these substances are meant to be used topically or internally for pet care. If your pet is sick or injured, please contact a vet or a qualified animal care specialist.

Keep any allergies in the household in mind when concocting your powders and oils. Wear protective gear when working with dangerous herbs, including safety glasses and a mask or bandana if needed. Avoid making or using powders if pregnant or nursing without first consulting a physician.

If you choose to use any of these substances in incense or a burning bowl, make sure that none of the substances produce harmful or irritating smoke (i.e. hydrangeas, chili peppers). Also, make sure you perform your burning out of doors or in a properly ventilated area. Observe all practical fire safety measures, and never leave a smoldering substance unattended. Never scatter powders containing salt onto grass or bare earth as it can cause harm to the vegetation and soil quality.

Always ensure that your magical oils and powders are properly stored. Glass is ideal, and any container you choose should have a tight-fitting lid in order to avoid spills or spoiling. Reclaimed food storage jars should be well-scrubbed and washed out with hot water and soap before being used to store powders or oils. Make sure all lingering food smells are gone, particularly from the lid, where stubborn sauces and sticky jellies can be difficult to remove. Oils should be stored somewhere dark and room-temperature or cooler for best preservation results. If you start to notice a rancid smell or odd things floating or growing in your oil, discard it and sanitize the container if you intend to use it again. Powders are a bit more forgiving; these can be stored in plastic if need be, though I don't recommend it over glass for bulk storage.

As with all things related to witchcraft, the frequent consultation and use of practical sources and common sense is strongly encouraged. Be smart. Be safe. Be sensible. And Happy Crafting!

Section One:

Magical Powders

All-Purpose Blessing Powder

For any magic or ritual involving blessing or consecration.

Ingredients:

- 2 pt Cedar
- 2 pt Rosemary
- 1 pt Bay Leaf
- 1 pt Clover
- 1 pt Lavender
- 1 pt Peppermint
- ½ pt Hyssop
- ½ pt Angelica Root
- ½ pt White Oak Bark
- ½ pt Black Walnut Hull

Use for any magic involving the blessing or consecration of items, spaces, or people. It is also useful for more general rituals related to blessing, even when they are not aimed at a particular physical target.

Pinches of this powder may be sprinkled in the corners of rooms or around the borders of a yard for general home blessing, or for consecration of a ritual space. Since there is no salt in the blend, the powder is safe to use on bare ground and should not pose a threat to your garden or lawn.

A spoonful of All-Purpose Blessing Powder may be mixed with an equal measure of powdered incense in your favorite scent and burnt for censing purposes. Be sure to cense only in well-ventilated areas or areas that can be easily cleared of smoke.

The powder can also be added to ornaments or charms made from wax or clay which are meant for long-term blessings given as gifts.

All-Purpose Cursing Powder

For all types of baneful magics from casual to severe.

Ingredients:

- 1 pt Cayenne Pepper
- 1 pt Black Pepper
- 1 pt White Pepper
- 1 pt Bloodroot**
- 1 pt Black Walnut Hull
- Pinch of Cinnamon
- Pinch of Cramp Bark
- Pinch of Nettle
- Pinch of Paprika
- Pinch of Onion Powder
- Pinch of Jalapeño Powder

This blend is all-purpose for baneful magic. Add to curse jars for an extra bite. Add to banishing spells that need to repel the unwanted subject with extreme prejudice. Drop a pinch in your enemy's yard or on their doorstep for instant casual cursing. Whisper the name of a person you want to curse and blow a small amount of powder downwind (so it doesn't come back in your face) to carry a jinx on the breeze.

Sprinkle a small amount into burning bowls or incenses for crossing, hexing, and ill-wishing. And when I say small amount, I mean a *small* amount. A tiny pinch of this powder goes a very long way. If you are going to use the powder in a burning bowl, you may want to omit the Jalapeño Powder, or use only in a well-ventilated area where you will not inhale the smoke.

Please note that some of these materials are irritants; do not inhale the powder or the smoke that rises from it, and do not add it to food or drink as a method of delivery.

All-Purpose Warding Powder

For all types of warding and protective barrier spells.

Ingredients:

- 2 pt Basil
- 2 pt Sage (any color)
- 1 pt Cedar Wood
- 1 pt Peppermint
- 1 pt Witch Hazel**
- 1 pt Willow Bark
- ½ pt Vetiver
- ½ pt Feverfew
- ½ pt Fennel
- Pinch of Black Pepper
- Pinch of Coriander or Cilantro

Use for any and all magics related to wards, barriers, threshold guards, property protection, or shielding spells.

Add a few pinches of All-Purpose Warding Powder to any homemade items tied to your household wards or protections. Some examples are witch bottles, ornament charms, charm bags or bottles, and wax charms. Store-bought and premade items make perfectly good anchors too. Just sprinkle a pinch of the powder over or into them before setting them in their appointed places. Refresh as needed.

I've found this powder to be effective when sprinkled across the top of a doorjamb or when used as an additive in a witch bottle. A prototype version of this powder also made a useful ingredient in a very basic "bedroom barrier" spell that I used to cast to help protect my privacy before I moved into my own apartment. The spell involved fusing a simple "Keep Out" charm into a spoonful of powder sprinkled across the doorway.

This powder makes an excellent ward enhancer for vehicles and luggage as well, if the more specialized Traveler's Luck Powder is not available.

Attraction Powder

For all-purpose attraction magic to bring you what you want.

Ingredients:

- 2 pt White Oak Bark
- 1 pt Bay Leaf Powder
- 1 pt Dill
- 1 pt Thyme
- ½ pt Calendula
- Pinch of Cardamom**
- Large Pinch of Iron Filings (per 1 cup batch)

Use for any magics to do with attraction. Keep in mind that attraction doesn't just have to do with love or romance. It can deal with wealth, employment, opportunities, or favorable circumstances.

This powder works exceptionally well when combined with melted beeswax and made into small charms. One quick method for making a personalized wax charm is to pour half a teaspoon's worth of melted wax combined with the desired powder onto foil or waxed paper. Let it cool until the edges begin to solidify and the wax becomes opaque, then make an impression with a metal stamp or your thumb. Be careful – it will still be fairly hot. Once the wax hardens completely, you will have a readymade charm suitable for inclusion in any spell you wish.

Note: If you intend to use this powder for incense or a burning bowl or candle seasoning, be aware that iron filings produce a shower of sparks when they come into contact with open flame. While this may not be enough to start an accidental fire, it may cause damage to your tools or your workspace. If you've prepared for this and want to add a little sparkle to your working, go for it. Just make sure you have an extinguisher handy in case something goes wrong. If you'd prefer to avoid the sparks, substitute a large pinch of Bergamot.

Beauty Salt

For general physical beauty spells and related glamours.

Ingredients:

- 3 pt Finely-Ground Salt
- 1 pt Talcum Powder
- 1 pt Magnolia Petals
- 1 pt Orange Peel
- ½ pt Petunia Blossoms
- ½ pt Myrtle Blossoms or Bark
- Few Drops of Evening Primrose Oil**

Note: If you are pregnant or nursing or have an allergy to Evening Primrose Oil, a few drops of Rose Oil may be substituted for scent. If you have an aversion to the scent of roses, use a few drops of your favorite perfume or cologne.

Place a small dish of Beauty Salt on your dresser or bathroom counter, wherever you perform your daily grooming routine. Add a small amount of Beauty Salt to any charm bottle used as an anchor for beauty glamours.

You can also use Beauty Salt for bath rituals. Place a tealight candle in a dish of Beauty Salt, and place the dish on your bathroom sink. Light the candle while you take your bath to activate and enhance the power of the salt. (The salt should not be used as a bath additive.)

Binding Powder

For all-purpose impediment of a target's ability to act.

Ingredients:

- 2 pt Marshmallow Root**
- 2 pt Sassafras Leaf
- 1 pt Orris Root
- 1 pt Calamus Root
- 1 pt Bloodroot**
- 1 pt Devil's Shoestring**
- ½ pt Solomon's Seal Root
- ½ pt Honeysuckle Flower

Use in magics intended to create or reinforce a binding spell, to impede movement, to prevent escape, to prevent actions or events, or to seal a charm or spell with especial strength.

Add this powder to any charm or spellwork related to binding, or to seal other types of spells and add to their tenacity. It's particularly well-suited to inclusion in paper packet bindings and poppet work. You can also put a pinch on somebody's shoes, or cast a palmful where you know they will walk.

In my workings, I've also found that rolling a string or piece of yarn in Binding Powder before use in any sort of impediment magic increases the spells' effectiveness and the speed with which it will act. It works best on poppets, but can also be used for jars or paper bundles.

Blocking Salt

To remove negativity from the environment.

Ingredients:

- 3 pt Salt
- 1 pt Dill
- 1 pt Rosemary
- 1 pt Willow Bark
- 1 pt Witch Hazel**
- ½ pt Elderflower (if desired)
- ½ pt Cinquefoil (if desired)

Place a small dish of Blocking Salt in any room where you feel the atmosphere is heavy or uncomfortable, as a simple cleansing measure. You can also sprinkle it in the corners of the room if there is a concern about the dish being disturbed by children or pets. The presence of the salt should work for about a month to keep the atmosphere clear of lingering negative or oppressive feelings.

If it's not practical to leave an open dish in the space or sprinkle the salt on the floor, you may want to employ a bottle or ornament charm. Fill the container partway with Blocking Salt, decorate it as you see fit, and place or hang it in the space.

Note: I've tried making this recipe with and without the Elderflower and Cinquefoil. I've found that it's more effective with the additional ingredients, in the sense that the atmosphere was cleared more quickly and stayed cleared for a longer period of time. The base mix worked just fine as well; it just took a day or so longer to fully clear the space. The overall effects lasted for a comparable amount of time once they were in place.

Bree's Banishing Powder

For wardings, banishings, and "GTFO" magics of all sorts.

Ingredients:

- 2 pt Cayenne Pepper
- 1 pt Cinnamon
- 1 pt Bree's Black Salt Blend
- ½ pt Black Pepper
- ½ pt Eggshell Powder

Use in the casting and reinforcement of home protection wards. Lay a few pinches just before your doorstep or across a threshold for a quick and easy defense against solicitors and unwanted guests. The same may be done after a house cleansing to prevent the return of ethereal pests.

The powder is also useful for any long-distance "stay away from me" spells. I highly recommend its' use in the removal of toxic persons from your life. It is particularly good for keeping away nosy or bothersome people, or an ex who just can't take a hint.

This is my Number One go-to magical powder. I often carry a vial of Banishing Powder in my pocket if I'm going somewhere that I feel edgy about, or if I know I'm going to be visiting a cemetery or any other place with heightened spirit activity. It is also a vital component in my annual warding ritual and every home cleansing that I perform.

Note: Will cause nasal irritation and much sneezing if inhaled. I have made this mistake many times. No matter how tempting the aroma, *do not* put your nose in the jar and sniff.

Bree's Black Salt Blend

For wardings, banishings, and protective barrier magic of all sorts.

Ingredients:

- 3 pt Ground Sea Salt (or Table Salt)
- 2 pt Oak Wood Charcoal
- 1 pt Burnt Protection Blend (see below)
- ½ pt Hawaiian Red Salt
- ½ pt Saltpeter

Protection Blend (dried for incense):

- 3 pt Green Sage
- 1 pt Sweet Basil
- 1 pt Rosemary
- 1 pt Cedar Tips
- ½ pt Blue Vervain
- Palmful of Cedar Chips (for kindling, as needed)

Burn a few teaspoons' worth of the Protection Blend to ashes. Let them cold completely before adding to the mortar or mixing bowl. Grind all the ingredients to powder separately, combine in a screw-top jar, and shake well until fully combined. If the blend looks too sooty, add more salt.

Black Salt can be used by itself for protective magics, or it can be added to other powders and charms to enhance their effectiveness. I also use it as a component in my Banishing Powder and occasionally as an additive to my All-Purpose Cursing Powder.

I've also found that if one happens to have troublesome neighbors, a pinch of Black Salt on your doorstep or pitched across the property line can encourage them to behave themselves…or at least leave you alone.

Word of Warning – This will stain your fingers soot black, along with anything else it touches. Use with caution.

Bree's Luck Salt

For attracting luck and good fortune.

Ingredients:

- 2 pt Salt
- 1 pt White Oak Bark
- 1 pt Ginger Root
- ½ pt Ground Allspice
- ½ pt Powdered Clover Leaf

Use in all magics intended to bring an upturn in luck. This salt makes a great additive for money-draw spells. Carry a pinch in the pocket or wallet to increase monetary wealth or bring luck in financial endeavors. Sprinkle a pinch in your shoes before embarking on any venture or occasion where fair fortune might be needed.

A small paper charm can be made with Luck Salt to help your savings or seed money grow. Sprinkle a pinch of Luck Salt onto a one-dollar bill (or comparable folding currency) and fold it into a packet so that the salt remains inside. Place the packet in your spare change jar or cashbox. This method also works well with Jackpot Powder.

Luck Salt is excellent for gamblers, job-seekers, and those whose occupations lie in the realm of finance. Scrub a pinch or two of salt between your palms before going into an important meeting or sitting down at the card table to turn the odds of victory and gain in your favor.

Business Blessing Powder

For general blessing of businesses and shops.

Ingredients:

- 2 pt Basil
- 1 pt Orange Peel
- 1 pt Patchouli
- 1 pt Willow Bark

Use in magics to protect and grow a business. This powder can help to increase good fortune, bring new opportunities, protect current investments, and prevent accidents.

A pinch or two tossed across your doorstep or workstation each week should be enough. You can also fill a small bottle or ornament with the powder and hang it over the door, or keep it in the cash register or your personal workspace. As with Bree's Luck Salt and Jackpot Powder, a dollar-bill charm packet with a few pinches of Business Blessing Powder can be kept in the cashbox or register, or with financial documents, to help the business grow.

This powder can also be used to bless business endeavors in which the caster is a participant, regardless of ownership. For use at a distance or for workings where it is not possible to directly deploy the powder, place a slip of paper bearing the legal name of the company, the persons involved in the venture, and any relevant details into a jar. Fill halfway with equal parts Business Blessing Powder and sugar. In cases where fundraising or venture capital is sought, place a lodestone or magnet on top of the jar to strengthen the spell.

Casting Salt

For an added power boost to any spell.

Ingredients:

- 3 pt Salt
- 1 pt Cinnamon
- 1 pt Cinquefoil
- 1 pt Ginger
- ½ pt Bergamot

Use to enhance or strengthen any spell or magical working. Casting Salt helps the effects of most spells to be stronger, more noticeable, and faster-acting.

Casting Salt does not always work as a booster for other powder-related spells, but it works particularly well for enhancing sigils or spoken spells. It can also be used to edge containment figures or as a supportive base for charms which may roll or become unsteady during castings.

I have used this powder as a shortcut to casting spells which are triggered by a word or incantation. A palmful of Casting Salt tossed out in front of oneself while the word or phrase is uttered usually does the trick.

Note: Do not use any powder containing salt on bare ground, as it causes harm to vegetation and soil quality.

Catalyst Spice Powder

To get things moving when they are stubborn or stagnant.

Ingredients:

- 1 pt Allspice
- 1 pt Cinnamon
- 1 pt Cloves
- 1 pt Ginger

This powder can be used to increase the vitality or speed with which a spell works, or to trigger or accelerate change.

Use in spellwork to set off certain effects or events, or to expedite an event. This powder can also be used to enhance the effect of any herbal charm blend to which it is added.

As it happens, Catalyst Spice is also an excellent flavoring for spice cakes, cookies, and certain fruit pies. This is one of the *only* powder recipes that I feel comfortable using as a food additive, but only if no one consuming the dish is allergic to the ingredients. This can be a tasty way to enhance your kitchen witchery and food magic, if you are so inclined.

For a quick and easy "make it happen" charm, combine a few pinches of Catalyst Spice Powder with a few drops of Posthaste Catalyst Oil, and squish the resulting paste into a small amount of salt dough or modeling clay as you contemplate what you want to happen. Form the clay into a ball and pierce it through with a chopstick or skewer, then allow the clay to dry. Hang the ball from the branch of a tree or shrub with a piece of sewing thread. Leave it there until the thread breaks and the ball drops, and then you will know that the result you hope for is soon to manifest. Make sure you retrieve the ball to prevent harm to the local plant life.

Clean House Powder

For regular home cleansing and magical maintenance.

Ingredients:

- 2 pt White Oak Bark
- 2 pt Sage (any color)
- 1 pt Lemon Peel
- 1 pt Cayenne Pepper
- 1 pt Plain Salt
- 1 pt Black Salt
- ½ pt Arrow Root
- ½ pt Blue Vervain
- ½ pt Solomon's Seal Root

Use in magics intended to cleanse a dwelling of negativity, "heaviness," bad energy, staleness, etc. Sprinkle a pinch in the corner of each room to dispel heaviness and clear the air, so to speak. Useful for spring cleaning and touch-up jobs throughout the year. Add to floor washes, incenses, or charms for general cleansing and purification of the home.

I've found that this powder is very effective for minor banishings as well, on the occasions when I find that a wayward spirit has wandered into my home. I also use it for periodic ward maintenance or simple one-step minor cleansings. A spoonful of powder added to a burning bowl makes for a quick and easy cleansing.

The use of a vacuum cleaner is advised if you dispense the powder on carpeted areas where small feet or paws might be running. The ingredients are not overtly harmful, but Cayenne Pepper can be irritating if it comes into contact with mucous membranes or sensitive skin.

Come Hither Powder

For attraction of love, romance, and sensual pleasures.

Ingredients:

- 2 pt Sugar
- 1 pt Savoury
- 1 pt Red Roses
- 1 pt Honeysuckle Blossom
- ½ pt Ginger Root
- ½ pt Lovage Herb
- ½ pt Poppy Seeds**
- 3 crushed Apple Seeds per ½ cup batch

Dust yourself very lightly with the powder before going to mixers or singles parties, or to any event where you feel you might meet someone exciting and attractive. If this is not your style, you can put a pinch in your shoes or carry a small bottle around your neck.

Cast a palmful into wind or fire on a full moon night to attract a lover. Add a spoonful to love incenses for a spicy-sweet kick to your liaisons. If you do this, make sure you omit the sugar.

Double the sugar and add olive oil to make a hand scrub for attracting a romantic partner. Do not, however, use this as an ingredient in massage oil.

This powder may be used to add a brief, adventurous zing to established relationships. Just make sure that all parties involved are aware and consenting, and be sure that you don't rely on it to keep things together once the high wears off.

Note: All love magic should be undertaken with great care. Do not use this powder to attempt to ensnare a specific person; it will not work. Be aware that the person you do attract may not be your ideal match. The love this powder attracts burns hot and fast, and it is not made to last forever. Use sparingly. Always protect yourself, employ common sense, and practice safe sex!

Cover My Tracks Powder

For deception and secrecy, when it is needed.

Ingredients:

- 1 pt Dogbane Leaves
- 1 pt Juniper Berries
- 1 pt Cherry Bark
- 1 pt Black Cohosh**
- ½ pt Poppy Seeds**

This powder is intended to hide one's intentions, actions, workings, or deeds when secrecy is required. Use in any magic where you need to work in secret, or where you need to conceal something that you said or did.

In general, you'll likely be using this powder for spells you cast on or about yourself. The easiest method is to focus on the deed or fact you wish to conceal, take a few steps, and toss a palmful of powder over your shoulder or scatter it behind you, figuratively covering your tracks. I suggest doing this outside as it makes a bit of a mess.

Cover My Tracks Powder is excellent for keeping secrets, for preventing discovery, for concealing items, or for warding spells designed to repel nosy housemates. A pinch of powder sprinkled across a doorway or near a hiding place is usually enough to suffice, as long as the powder doesn't make the hidden item obvious.

As with Invisibility Powder and Obfuscation Powder, a pinch or so in your shoes can help you pass unnoticed if need be. This is not foolproof, but it can help. It also counters Notice Me Powder if you're feeling too visible.

Curseturner Powder

To turn the effects of baneful magic back upon its' caster.

Ingredients:

- 1 pt Basil (any type)
- 1 pt Rosemary
- 1 pt White Willow Bark
- 1 pt Angelica Root
- ½ pt Witch Hazel**
- ½ pt Hyssop
- ½ pt Bloodroot**
- ½ pt Cascara Segrada

Use in magics intended to remove the effects of harmful magic and turn it back on the person who cast it. Burn with incense to negate and counter hexes, curses, or ill-wishing laid upon you or another. Cleanse yourself after use.

The ill effects should dissipate within three days and rebound upon the person who cast the baneful magic, known or unknown.

One method I've found to be effective is to acquire a cheap mirrored blush compact, empty out the makeup, and replace it with a spoonful of Curseturner Powder mixed with beeswax or coconut oil. The presence of the mirror enhances the powder's efficacy, and creates an instant pocket charm that's easy to carry with you.

For best results, make sure that you pair the use of this powder with a strengthening or recasting of your household protections, and a decided effort in your mundane life to distance yourself from the person who is hexing you, if the party is known.

Dead Man's Dust Powder

For preventing spirits from following you home.

Ingredients:

- 1 pt Chili Pepper (any type)
- 1 pt Salt
- 1 pt Basil
- 1 pt Garlic Powder
- ½ pt Dill
- ½ pt Lemon Peel

Optional: Add a pinch of Curry or Cumin for extra oomph.

This powder performs one of the functions of Banishing Powder, but with special attention to warding off pesky ghosts.

After visiting historical or haunted locations, or any time you feel spooked while walking home, sprinkle a palmful of powder on the ground and scrape your feet on it (as if you were wiping off dirt) to keep anything ghostly from following you home. Take three steps backward and spit toward the powder, then continue on your way.

For extra protection, toss a pinch of Banishing Powder, Threshold Powder, or Black Salt over your doorstep when you get home.

Note: For safety's sake, make sure you never cast this powder into the wind and wash your hands after use. Leftover particles on your skin can cause pain and irritation if they come into contact with your eyes or breathing passages.

Deflection Salt

To divert bad luck or baneful magics.

Ingredients:

- 3 pt Salt
- 1 pt Agrimony**
- 1 pt Bloodroot**
- 1 pt Sage (any color)
- ½ pt Fennel
- ½ pt Marjoram

Use in any magic intended to prevent bad luck or magical harm via deflection, as opposed to nullifying or countering. Think of it like the magical equivalent of an umbrella. The "rain," as it were, is directed away from you and into neutral territory without risk to innocent bystanders.

A small bottle of Deflection Salt hung from your car's rearview mirror or tucked into the glove box may help prevent accidents and mishaps on long trips, particularly when paired with safe driving. A pinch or two of the powder in a protection charm will have the same effect.

If you are concerned about baneful magics being directed at your person, a pendant charm containing Deflection Salt may come in handy.

Done Deal Powder

For assisting and augmenting negotiations, especially where finances or legal matters are involved.

Ingredients:

- 2 pt Sugar
- 1 pt Thyme
- 1 pt Cinnamon
- ½ pt Bergamot
- ½ pt Buttercup Petals
- ½ pt Sumac Berries

Use this powder in any magic designed to increase the likelihood of negotiations, debates, or discussions going your way. It is particularly useful for brokering business deals, asking for raises, settling internal workplace disputes, and improving the chances that court cases or legal battles will be decided in your favor.

Dust your hands lightly with the powder before going into meetings or discussions. Drop a few pinches into your shoes before a court date. To help others in these situations, write down the person's name and a brief description of how they want the situation to go, then roll up the paper and stick it in a small jar of Done Deal Powder.

For stronger control of the situation, add ½ pt Sassafras Leaf or Root, or non-smoking Tobacco Leaf if it is available.

Dream Dust

For dreams and visions; for restful sleep with pleasant dreams.

Ingredients:

- 2 pt Marjoram
- 1 pt Hibiscus Flower
- 1 pt Jasmine Flower
- 1 pt Valerian**
- ½ pt Poppy Flower* **
- ½ pt Vervain

Use in magics intended to bring pleasant dreams, banish nightmares, and ensure a restful night's sleep. This powder can also be used in any magic related to sleep or dreaming, including (but not limited to) dream-sending, dream manipulation, and protection from nightmares while sleeping.

To make a dream doll for sympathetic magic, mix a few pinches of powder with soft clay or melted candle wax and form the substance into a small human figure. Name the figurine for the person it is meant to protect, wrap it in cotton cloth, and tuck it under the mattress.

To increase the probability of prophetic dreams or visions, a small amount of Dream Dust may be combined with powdered incense and burnt before retiring to bed. Do not directly inhale large amounts of the smoke, and do not use this method if you are pregnant or nursing.

"Eye of Sauron" Revelation Powder

To force a liar out of hiding and expose their misdeeds and trickery.

Ingredients:

- 2 pt Galangal Root
- 1 pt Deer's Tongue Herb
- 1 pt Black Sugar
- 1 pt Black Salt
- 1 pt Ground Pumice
- Pinch of Copal Resin
- Pinch of Dragon's Blood Resin

Use in magics intended to reveal lies and dishonesty, or to reveal a liar or deceitful person to the eyes of the world.

Sprinkle where you know your target will walk, or across the entrance to a room or dwelling, or in the corners of a room. (The powder is most effective when trodden upon by the target.) As you do so, visualize a flaming eye stripping away their lies and dishonesty.

For creating the effect at a distance, burn a pinch of powder with a slip of paper bearing the target's name or image.

Black sugar may be obtained from some shops that sell baking decorations, particularly around the Halloween season. If it is not available in your area, regular white sugar mixed with charcoal may be substituted.

Note: This powder has no association with the works of J.R.R. Tolkien beyond the inspiration for the name.

Find-A-Friend Powder

For attracting and maintaining friendships.

Ingredients:

- 2 pt Confectioner's Sugar
- 1 pt Forget-Me-Not Blossoms
- 1 pt Pink Rose Petals
- 1 pt Meadowsweet**
- ½ pt Passionflower Herb**
- ½ pt Cloves

This blend is useful for attracting platonic companionship. The principles and methodology of such spells are largely the same as spells for romantic attraction. The main difference is in the intent, where you'd focus on attracting a friend or a partner rather than a lover or a spouse.

Find-A-Friend Powder is excellent for practitioners looking for everything from casual lunch buddies to partners for spellwork to roommates to your new best friend. Use it to fill a paper charm that contains a list of desirable traits, or to fill a dish supporting a candle carved for an attraction spell.

Add the powder to a bottle charm that you carry with you to attract quality friends and companions. You can also combine it with modeling clay and use that to create a charm or poppet to be the focus of such spells.

Get Thee Hence Powder

For getting rid of stubborn ex-lovers, or would-be suitors who don't understand the meaning of "no." Counters Come Hither Powder, should the need arise.

Ingredients:

- 1 pt Pistachio Shells
- 1 pt Lime Peel
- 1 pt Cinnamon
- ½ pt Lemon Verbena
- ½ pt Black Pepper
- ½ pt Witch Hazel**
- 3 crushed Chili Pepper seeds per 1-cup batch (any type)

Optional: If the lover in question was attracted by magic, add ½ part Turmeric.

To rid yourself of a persistent ex, bind up three generous pinches in brown paper upon which is written your ex-lover's name, tie with black string, and bury the packet under a flat stone somewhere off your property. If you can do so under a thorny bush or shrub, so much the better.

If your problem is harassment at school or in the workplace or a social setting, carry a small packet or bottle of the powder with you, or sprinkle several pinches where you know the person is certain to walk over it. To sever the attachment and put an end to things, dust your hands with the powder and firmly shake hands with the target while saying goodbye in some fashion. (Make sure it's "goodbye" or "farewell," not "see you later" or the like. Do not wash your hands until after the handshake.)

If your problem is unwanted attention at your home, sprinkle three pinches at each corner of your property, then mix a spoonful of the powder with 2 cups of vinegar and use it to wash your doorstep.

Ghost-Be-Gone Powder

To banishing interloping spirits.

Ingredients:

- 2 pt Angelica Root
- 2 pt Basil (any type)
- 1 pt White Oak Bark
- 1 pt White Willow Bark
- ½ pt Bloodroot**
- ½ pt Black Salt
- ½ pt Sandalwood (if desired)

Use in magics intended to remove troublesome spirits from your home. Sprinkle in the corners of each room, and across thresholds and windowsills to banish unwanted spirits and prevent their return.

Cast a few pinches of Ghost-Be-Gone Powder out your front door or on your doorstep after performing a home cleansing or banishing ritual to help keep your home free of uninvited spirits. Keep a bottle of the powder in troublesome areas to help reduce problems with mild to moderate hauntings and make any spirits who wander in easier to remove. Including the powder in regular cleansing rituals also helps to keep out all but the most determined metaphysical pests.

Add a small amount of Sandalwood or your preferred incense powder to create a burnable mix for smoke-cleansing purposes. Be sure to ventilate your home well after censing as part of a spell or ritual.

Harmony Salt

To create peaceful and harmonious environments.

Ingredients:

- 3 pt Salt
- 1 pt Lavender
- 1 pt Sweet Basil
- 1 pt Catnip or Lemon Balm
- 1 pt White Rose Petals
- ½ pt Cherry Blossoms
- ½ pt Marjoram

Use to promote peacefulness in one's room or the entire home. This salt is also useful for ritual and meditation spaces, though it should not be sprinkled on bare ground due to the risk of harming the soil and vegetation

The method I most recommend is to put several spoonfuls of Harmony Salt into a small dish and place the dish in the space where you seek to promote an atmosphere of tranquility. It is best to make sure the dish is out of the reach of children and pets to reduce the risk of spills. The salt can then be changed every month or two to keep the effects fresh.

Note: I have tried making this particular salt two ways, with Catnip and with Lemon Balm, and both blends worked equally well for my purposes. If you have both herbs available, I do recommend trying this both ways before deciding which one to use. An equal-parts blend of Catnip and Lemon Balm can also be used if you prefer not to experiment.

Heal Thy Body Powder

For assistance with physical healing.

Ingredients:

- 2 pt White Willow Bark
- 1 pt Feverfew
- 1 pt Sage (any color)
- 1 pt Horehound Herb
- ½ pt Apple Leaf
- ½ pt Sassafras Leaf
- ½ pt Blue Vervain
- Pinch of Arrow Root
- Pinch of Sheep Sorrel
- Pinch of Oregon Grape Root**

Use in magics intended to relieve pain, illness, weakness, fatigue, or other physical ailments, including paper charms or healing poppet spells.

For a simple healing spell, a poppet named for the ailing person may be sprinkled with Heal Thy Body Powder, concentrating on the areas that require healing. If you don't happen to have a poppet handy, a fingerling potato works very well as a substitute. A paper packet inscribed with the patient's name and the ailment to be healed can be used in a similar way.

The ingredients for this powder address a number of different physical ailments and conditions, and most are associated with mundane healing as well as magical. However, keep in mind that this powder is not meant to replace modern medical treatment and should not be applied topically or internally.

Heal Thy Heart Powder

For emotional healing and relief of heartache.

Ingredients:

- 2 pt Red Roses
- 1 pt Witch Hazel**
- 1 pt Orange Peel
- 1 pt Cherry Bark
- ½ pt Coriander
- ½ pt Cinnamon
- Pinch of Ground Cloves

Use in magics intended to relieve heartache, heartbreak, loneliness, grief, and other emotional pains. Use in any spellwork likewise designed to ease pains of the heart, be they from loss, fatigue, relationships, or general sadness. Add to charms to help oneself or another recover from any emotional pain.

Heal Thy Heart Powder makes an excellent additive for wax or clay charms, or as an ingredient in incense meant to cleanse sadness and grief from your home. (I suggest Amber or Frankincense powder for the base.)

To create a bottle charm for emotional healing, put several generous pinches of Heal Thy Heart Powder into a small bottle. Add a strand of your hair, a fingernail clipping, or a few tears. Close the bottle and hold it over your chest so that the contents are stirred by your heartbeat. Do this for seven days during a waning moon, then discard the powder by burial or burning.

Note: Please remember to practice self care and seek outside support when you find yourself in need during your recovery. If you are in a dangerous or harmful situation, remove yourself to safe place if you are able.

Hexbreaker Powder

To break or remove baneful magic.

Ingredients:

- 1 pt Angelica Root
- 1 pt Galangal Root
- 1 pt Cayenne Pepper
- 1 pt Powdered Nutmeg
- 1 pt Garlic Powder
- ½ pt Black Pepper
- ½ pt Nettle Leaf
- ½ pt Solomon's Seal Root

Use in magics intended to break, remove, or otherwise nullify a curse, jinx, hex, ill-wishing, or any baneful magic. This also counters the effects of All-Purpose Cursing Powder, should the need arise.

Use for any spellwork designed to remove or prevent magical harm. The powder works equally well on persons and dwellings, and is generally intended for use on baneful magics with a relatively recent origin. It's most effective within one lunar month of the date that you first notice symptoms of possible baneful influence.

And yes, you can still use it as a precautionary measure if you're not sure. Determining whether you're cursed or not is a difficult and highly subjective business, and sometimes it's best to just take corrective or preventative action and have done with the matter.

If you suspect a long-standing curse on your family or property whose noticeable effects have lasted for more than a year, you may want to seek the assistance of a specialist if you're going to try to remove it. There may be historical factors at work that should be considered in the procedure.

Hold Strong Powder

To increase strength and tenacity of any spell.

Ingredients:

- 2 pt Black Tea Leaf
- 1 pt Tangerine Peel
- 1 pt Cinnamon
- ½ pt Marigold Petals (Calendula)
- ½ pt Red Carnation Petals
- 1 Powdered Orchid Blossom per batch (if available)

Use to increase willpower in situations where you find you need to stand your ground or put your foot down. Use in any spellwork for this purpose. This powder can also be used to increase the strength and tenacity of any spell, if you want the effects to be very emphatic or last for a long time.

The ideal application for this powder is in a binding. It will work as an additive to just about any kind of spell, but I've found that using a binding as the method of delivery follows the intent in a logical manner and makes for easy casting. This can be done as part of the initial spell or as a separate casting that you do later on, whichever works best for you.

The powder can also be used to quickly and temporarily bolster the strength of long-term spells which are fading. For example, to shore up your household protections without recasting them, create a quick witch web with a small embroidery hoop and whatever color of string resonates with you. Once the web is finished, use a paintbrush to lightly coat the strands with glue.

Spread a few spoonfuls of Hold Strong Powder on a paper plate. Add some glitter for extra color, if you like. Then place the embroidery hoop flat on the plate and gently shake it around so that the powder adheres to the strands of the web. Repeat on both sides, tap to remove excess powder, and let it dry. Decorate the web as you seek fit and hang it in your window or near your front door.

Home Blessing Powder

For general home blessing spells.

Ingredients:

- 1 pt Angelica Root
- 1 pt Orange Peel
- 1 pt Blue Vervain
- ½ pt White Willow Bark
- ½ pt Black Pepper
- ½ pt Dill

Use in spells to bless and protect the home and its' occupants. Technically, this could be labeled another "all-purpose" powder, as it is useful for all blessing spells that deal with the homestead and members of the household.

The easiest way to use Home Blessing powder is to create a charm bottle. Fill a small bottle with the powder as you meditate on all the good things you wish to keep in your home. Seal the bottle with wax and your thumbprint and keep it on somewhere that it won't be disturbed. Some ideas include the mantel, the altar, or a curio cabinet. The witch web project listed on the previous page might be something else to try.

If you prefer, you can sprinkle small amount of the powder on top of the lintel of your front door. The lintel is crossbar created by the molding on top of the doorjamb. You can also add the powder to ornament charms or to censing blends for blessing your new place.

Honest Passion Powder

For increasing consensual passion, devotion, and happiness in a romantic relationship.

Ingredients:

- 1 pt Bloodroot**
- 1 pr Red Roses
- 1 pt Rose-scented Incense Powder
- ½ pt Hibiscus Flower
- ½ pt Jezebel Root
- ½ pt Cherry Bark
- ½ pt Red Clover
- Pinch of Dragon's Blood

Sprinkle a pinch in the corners of your bedroom to increase happiness and passion. Use in any spellwork related to fidelity, increased devotion, better communication, or re-connecting with your partner(s).

Burn as you would any powdered incense for these purposes as well. If you wish to use the powder as incense, you may want to add just a pinch or two more Rose or Dragon's Blood incense powder and mix well to help it burn more completely.

Remember to reinvest in your relationship in a mundane sense in conjunction with the use of this powder. Communication and respect are key!

Inspiration Salt

To increase creativity and inventiveness.

Ingredients:

- 3 pt Salt
- 1 pt Horehound
- 1 pt Jasmine
- ½ pt Allspice
- ½ pt Witch Hazel**

Use in any and all magics meant to stimulate innovative thinking or inspire new ideas. If you are a witch with a creative side or lots of term papers to finish, this salt just might be your new best friend.

Place a small bowl of Inspiration Salt in workspace to encourage new ideas. If you are inclined to candle magic, you can place a tealight candle in the center of the dish to amplify the salt's effects. (Open flame is not required to make this work; a battery-operated LED candle can provide the necessary amplification if needed.) If a candle is not available, a lodestone works well too.

Inspiration Salt makes a good additive for clay charms if you're in the mood to make salt dough clay. A small "study buddy" may be crafted to sit on your desk and lighten your work sessions.

Instant Glamour Powder

For creating and activating simple physical glamour magics.

Ingredients:

- 1 pt Black Tea Leaves
- 1 pt Orange Peel
- 1 pt Ground Allspice
- ½ pt Petunia Blossoms
- ½ pt Potato Flour or Starch
- ½ pt Sugar

Use this powder for any glamour which is meant to affect or alter your physical appearance. This includes beauty glamours, disguise glamours, invisibility glamours, and presentation glamours.[1]

I've found that the most effective applications involve paper charms with your name or a personal taglock included. One simple method is to write your name and the desired effect of the glamour on a small piece of paper, then cover it with a pinch of Instant Glamour powder, roll it up, and seal it with wax or tape.

When you need the effect of the glamour, snap the paper tube and sprinkle the powder around you in a circle. You can even color-code the tubes for different glamours. (Just be careful if you're carrying white ones, as they may resemble an illegal substance.)

If you'd rather leave the paper charm at home, include a strand of hair or a nail clipping before you seal up the paper tube, and tuck the charm away somewhere that it won't be disturbed.

---

[1] Glamours which encourage the onlooker to perceive and address you as you wish to be perceived and addressed.

Inversion Powder

To reverse the intent or usage of any powder, herb mixture, or physical charm to which it is added.

Ingredients:

- 1 pt Ash of Roses
- 1 pt Charcoal

Use as a simple method to invert the intent or usage of a spell which employs powder, herb blends, or a physical charm. For example, a fidelity charm would become a curse of betrayal; a shielding blend would become a ward breaker; a cursing blend would become a protection against the malady the curse was meant to invoke. This can become problematic and complicated in a hurry, and should be used with caution. Be sure that you close the loopholes in your spell to prevent unwanted side effects.

Inversion Powder can also be used to bind harmful people or situations, particularly where magic or intrigue is being leveled against you. Inverting intentions, attitudes, or situations can be a little tricky, but if you succeed, it's well worth it.

To invert a situation, get a piece of paper and write a description of what's going on. Smear the words with Inversion Powder until they are obscured; the charcoal and ash make this fairly easy. If necessary, make a paste using a few drops of water and then apply it like fingerpaint. Fold the paper up, tape the edges, and rewrite the situation on the outside of the packet, describing how you would like things to go. Store the packet somewhere safe until matters improve.

To invert a person's intentions or attitude, or to counter magic being used against you, use the method described above to blacken a paper poppet named for the offending party. Then fold the poppet up and black it with white thread or twine. For extra measure, you can stick the bound poppet into a sweetening jar with sugar or Sweetening Powder. Leave it there until the desired effect is achieved.

Invisibility Powder

For perceived invisibility.

Ingredients:

- 2 pt Poppy Seeds**
- 1 pt Chicory Root
- 1 pt Valerian**
- Cornstarch (as needed)

Note: This powder does not actually make you invisible; it is meant to grant perceived invisibility, which is a minor glamour that helps you remain unnoticed so long as you do not overtly call attention to yourself. If you are in a dangerous situation, make sure that you take all practical measures to protect yourself.

Use in magics intended to help the caster pass unseen, disappear into the background, or escape the notice of hostile parties. Put a pinch in your shoes to help carry you through the day. This powder is also useful in anti-bullying spells where passing a person or place unseen may keep you safe.

Be careful when using this powder. Do not use it in or around your car. Make sure you remove or counter the glamour before going anywhere that perceived invisibility might be detrimental, such as an important meeting, a competition, or a road trip.

Invisibility Powder can be countered by Notice Me Powder. Perceived invisibility glamours may be removed by washing off the powder and dressing or acting in a way that draws the positive attention of others.

Jackpot Powder

To bring monetary wealth or a financial boost.

Ingredients:

- 1 pt Ground Allspice
- 1 pt Fenugreek
- 1 pt Cinnamon
- ½ pt Goldenseal*
- ½ pt Dragon's Blood

* - Substitute Oregon Grape Root if possible. Goldenseal is rare and expensive, while Oregon Grape Root is cheaper and more sustainable, though it should be avoided if you are pregnant or nursing.

Use in magics intended to draw wealth to the caster. Sprinkle a pinch over a green candle when working wealth magic, or add to a folded paper packet and place in a jar of spare change to help boost your finances. You can also put a pinch in your shoes before asking for a raise, or dust your hands with it before gambling.

The powder can be burnt as incense during spellwork for drawing fast money.

A small paper charm can be made with Jackpot Powder to help your savings or seed money grow. Sprinkle a pinch of Jackpot Powder onto a one-dollar bill (or comparable folding currency) and fold it into a packet so that the salt remains inside. Place the packet in your spare change jar or cashbox. This method also works well with Bree's Luck Salt.

Jar of Dirt Protection Powder

For compact, portable home protection.

Ingredients:

- 1 cup of Dry Soil from Your Home (or a place of power)
- Equal Parts:
  Angelica Root
  Basil
  Cedar Wood
  Horehound
  Juniper
  Peppermint
  Rosemary
  White Oak Bark
  Witch Hazel**

Combine the ingredients and mix well, then divide equally between two small jars with tight-fitting lids. Leave one in your home where it will not be disturbed, and take the other with you when you travel for extended periods.

This is equal parts usable powder and ready-made protection spell. Pinches of powder from either jar may be used for home protection spells, or for on-to-go protection spells while traveling. The soil ties the jars to your home protection measures, so the stronger you can make them, the stronger the portable protection will be.

Jinx Salt

To augment the casting of casual baneful magic spells.

Ingredients:

- 3 pt Salt
- 1 pt Chili Powder
- 1 pt Paprika
- ½ pt Lime Peel
- ½ pt Lemon Grass

This salt is intended for small jinxes and casual cursing. Most baneful spells of this sort can be accomplished with simple words or gestures, but Jinx Salt can give them a little extra punch. Use it for small baneful magics performed at home; carrying a bottle around in case you need to hex somebody can be a bit of a pain.

Add a pinch or two of Jinx Salt to low-level curse jars to give them a particular bite. A bit of the salt pressed into a clay poppet or sealed up in a paper charm works well for short-term hexes or spells to cause the subject minor irritations or bad luck.

For a quick and easy jinx, whisper your intentions to a palmful of Jinx Salt, then scatter it where you know the target will walk. Take care that the subject will be the next person to walk over the area or the jinx could be diluted or dispersed by passersby.

Note: Do not throw Jinx Salt at the subject of your hex or add it to their food or drink. This salt is for indirect magical use *only*.

Jobfinder Powder No. 1

To assist with finding gainful employment quickly.

Ingredients:

- 1 pt Sweet Basil
- 1 pt Hawthorn
- 1 pt Meadowsweet**
- 1 pt Thyme
- ½ pt Oregon Grape Root**

Use in magics intended to help one find or gain employment.

Put a pinch in each shoe before going to a job interview. Fold some powder up in a sheet of paper with your resume printed on it. Carry the packet with you while job-hunting.

Jobfinder Powder No. 2

To assist with finding long-term, career-oriented employment.

Ingredients:

- 1 pt Black Pepper
- 1 pt Ground Cloves
- 1 pt Ginger Root
- 1 pt Gravel Root
- 1 pt Lavender
- 1 pt Roses

Use in magics intended to help one find or gain employment.

This version of the powder is more suited to finding a career than just a job for the short term. It is also useful for spells intended to help one keep a job if there is some indication that a layoff is imminent.

Lion's Roar Powder

For general confidence and courage-bringing magic. Also useful for non-physical glamours of the same kind.

Ingredients:

- 2 pt Lady's Mantle**
- 1 pt Dandelion Blossom
- 1 pt Sunflower Petals
- 1 pt Marigold Petals
- ½ pt Witch Hazel**
- ½ pt Ground Cloves

Use in magic designed to help increase confidence, instill courage, and help you maintain a brave face through difficult situations.

Sprinkle a pinch in your shoes or dust a scapegoat with the powder before leaving for the day. If you feel you may need additional help throughout the day, bring along a small vial of the powder. Cast a palmful on the ground and scrape your feet on it to banish fear and give your bravery a boost. To assist this, visualize the presence of a roaring lion, whether made of your personal energy or as a companion animal, and picture the sound of the roar scattering all that which would frighten you.

Throw a palmful over your tracks to keep fear from following you home. This is especially helpful for people who experience anxiety at school or in the workplace or on public outings. While this method cannot treat anxiety-related disorders, as a ritual it may help you separate yourself from places which are sources of fear and discomfort before returning to your personal sanctuary.

For ongoing confidence glamours, mix the powder with melted wax and your favorite scented oil and create a solid perfume. Beeswax or soy wax works best for this, since it's less likely to irritate the skin. Apply a small amount to your pulse points when casting or refreshing non-physical confidence-related glamours.

Long Haul Powder

To enable spells to keep their potency for longer periods of time.

Ingredients:

- 1 pt Black Tea Leaves
- 1 pt Thyme
- 1 pt Vervain
- 1 pt Spearmint
- ½ pt Anise
- ½ pt Oak Bark

Use this powder as an additive in spells which must work for a long time, or cumulatively over a period of time. It can also be used to strengthen various spells and charms, and help them last longer than they otherwise might. This is very useful for heavy-duty protection spells which must be trusted to hold against strong opposition.

The powder is also effective for spells which must work at a great distance. Usually, the constraints of geography do not affect the results of a spell, but I have found that if certain spells must travel several hundred miles to find their target, their efficacy may to suffer. Adding a pinch of Long Haul Powder can help the spell get to its' target intact.

Love-Me Powder

To augment the casting of consensual love magics.

Ingredients:

- 2 pt Red Rose Petals
- 1 pt Strawberry Leaf
- 1 pt Feverfew
- 1 pt Jasmine
- ½ pt Meadowsweet**
- ½ pt Lady's Mantle**
- Pinch of Crushed Strawberry Seeds
- Pinch of Crushed Poppy Seeds**

Note: The inclusion of the word "consensual" in the description above is very deliberate. Love magic, if it is to work properly and ethically, must not infringe upon the free will of the parties involved. *Never* try to force someone into a romantic or sexual relationship against their will, either through magic or mundane means.

Blow a palmful of Love-Me Powder out of your window before bedtime to bring dreams of love to yourself or to send them to your sweetheart…or to someone who would like to fill the role. Add the powder to household charms designed to preserve or refresh existing love, such as an ornament or a red wax heart. For extra sweetness, you can use scented wax or add a drop of Strawberry fragrance oil.

Mix Love-Me Powder with Rose-scented incense for censing or love incenses. This incense works very well for helping couple reconcile after arguments or just rekindling that spark when things have gotten stale. It's also great as an accompaniment for spells designed to attract someone special into your life.

To create Love-Me-Not Salt, which negates love magic and repels unwanted affection, add 1 pt Love-Me Powder to 2 pt Salt and 1 pt Ash of Roses. Use this in banishing spells or to break pre-existing love charms.

Lover-Be-True Powder

To increase fidelity in romantic relationships.

Ingredients:

- 2 pt Red Rose Petals
- 1 pt Jezebel Root
- 1 pt Hydrangea Blossom
- 1 pt Magnolia Blossom
- ½ pt White Rose Petals
- ½ pt Strawflower

Use in magics intended to prevent wandering eyes and hands, to keep a lover faithful, or to ward off the attentions of one who would attempt to seduce your lover or spouse. Add to fidelity spells to keep a lover from straying, or to binding or banishing spells to get rid of an interloper or remind handsy acquaintances to keep their paws to themselves.

This powder can also be used to help one's own eyes from straying, if that is a concern. Remember to double down on this by communicating openly and reinvesting in your relationship as often as possible.

Note: *Do not burn this powder or use it in incense*, due to the toxic properties of the smoke that comes from burning Hydrangea. If you absolutely must use fire for a love spell, either leave the Hydrangea out of your blend, or choose another powder altogether. Safety First!

Lucky Day Powder

For one full day (24 hours) of increased good fortune.

Ingredients:

- 1 pt Orange Peel
- 1 pt Fenugreek
- 1 pt Ginger Root
- 1 pt Lemon Peel
- ½ pt Cinnamon
- ½ pt Irish Moss

Use in magics intended to bring good luck and high probability of success to follow for one full day. Put a pinch in your shoes before going out on any day that you need a boost of good fortune, or chance to sway in your favor. This powder is also useful for spellwork related to finding or keeping employment and obtaining wealth.

The powder can also be added to money-drawing and good-fortune incenses, or sprinkled into burning bowls put together for the same purpose.

Add to incense and charms designed to bring luck. Combine in a jar with sesame seeds for long-term household use. (The latter method delivers a quick boost which then tapers off over time.)

Nightmare Dust

To produce bad dreams and night terrors.

Ingredients:

- 2 pt Nettle Leaf
- 2 pt Cramp Bark
- 2 pt Black Salt
- 1 pt Mullein Leaf
- 1 pt Poppy Flower* **
- ½ pt Wormwood* **

Use in magics intended to curse a target with bad dreams and sleepless nights. Sprinkle the powder beneath the target's bed or employ in a poppet, curse jar, or paper charm to bring insomnia, anxiety, fear, poor sleep, restlessness, and nightmares.

As with Dream Dust, you can mix a bit of Nightmare Dust into clay or melted wax to create a poppet for sympathetic magic, or roll it up in a slip of paper bearing the target's name.

Note: Exercise special caution when preparing and using this powder. Wormwood is a poisonous herb, and if inhaled in sufficient quantities, it can be hallucinogenic or toxic. I do not recommend using it in incense form. Do not ingest or inhale the powder, or administer to anyone in food or drink; do not apply it directly to pillows or bedclothes either. If you are allergic to Wormwood or Ragweed, avoid preparing this recipe altogether.

Notice Me Powder

To make oneself more visible.

Ingredients:

- 1 pt Primrose**
- 1 pt Pennyroyal**
- 1 pt Sumac Berries
- ½ pt Sandalwood
- ½ pt Vetiver

Use in magics intended to make oneself stand out or be noticed. Also counters the effects of Invisibility Power and Obfuscation Powder, should the need arise.

Notice Me Powder is highly useful when you need to stand out from the crowd in career or competition. When you need to shine just a little bit brighter than the people around you, put a pinch in your shoes or cast it over your shoulder before you strut your stuff.

This applies to everyday matters as well. If you feel that you just aren't getting enough attention or aren't being taken as seriously as you'd like, create a paper charm with a few pinches of Notice Me Powder and the names or titles of the people who need to stop brushing you off.

Be aware that you may attract unwanted attention, so have countermeasures ready if the spotlight becomes too much to handle. Invisibility Powder and Cover My Tracks Powder work well for this, should the need arise.

Note: Do not prepare or use this powder if you are pregnant or are trying to become so, due to the presence of Primrose and Pennyroyal. The latter in particular poses a significant risk and should be avoided during pregnancy.

Obfuscation Powder

To confuse and bewilder, to prevent detection or discovery, or to make oneself inconspicuous.

Ingredients:

- 2 pt Dogbane
- 2 pt Sumac Berries
- 2 pt Juniper Berries
- 1 pt Boneset
- 1 pt Mistletoe* **
- 1 pt Bloodroot**

Use in magics intended to confuse or stupefy a foe, or to prevent discovery of secrets or deeds. Add to spells meant to disguise or deceive, particularly where it applies to keeping someone from finding out what you've done or what you're up to.

Obfuscation Powder differs from Cover My Tracks Powder and Invisibility Powder in that it is intended not just to conceal what needs concealing, but also to cause confusion and uncertainty. Think of it as the magical equivalent of a smoke bomb.

Carry a small vial in your pocket when you need to be inconspicuous or make a quick getaway, or put a pinch in your shoes when you wish to leave no trace of where you've been. This powder may also be used in cursing or binding to dull someone's wits or perceptions.

Outta My Way Powder

For removing obstacles to success in your personal or professional life.

Ingredients:

- 1 pt Sumac Berries
- 1 pt Galangal Root
- 1 pt White Oak Bark
- 1 pt Black Sugar
- ½ pt Sassafras Leaf
- ½ pt Ground Cloves
- ½ pt Jalapeño Powder

Use in magics intended to remove difficult obstacles caused by other people. Sprinkle the powder where you know the person who is the cause of your problem will be walking.

Alternatively, you can write down a list of your grievances, the method by which you want the obstacle removed, and the ideal outcome; then add a few pinches of the powder and fold the paper into a tight packet, using tape if necessary. Stick the packet in a spell jar or carry it in your pocket, whichever is more relevant to your situation.

Black sugar may be obtained from some shops that sell baking decorations, particularly around the Halloween season. If it is not available in your area, regular white sugar mixed with charcoal may be substituted.

Paper Tiger Powder

To neutralize a threat and remove their power.

Ingredients:

- 1 pt Cedar
- 1 pt Dried Onion
- 1 pt Tea Leaf
- ½ pt Bloodroot**
- ½ pt Ash of Roses

Note: For those not familiar with the phrase, a paper tiger someone or something which appears to be powerful or dangerous, but is actually weak and ineffectual.

Use in magics intended to reduce a person's power to harm you or interfere with your life, or to reveal a puffed-up braggart for the blustering coward that they are.

This powder works best in sympathetic magic worked at a distance, with a poppet or paper charm. I suggest starting with your favorite binding spell and going from there. It is also effective as a strew when placed where you know the target will walk.

Peacekeeper Powder

To quell arguments and prevent conflict.

Ingredients:

- 2 pt Coriander Seed
- 1 pt Black Walnut Hull
- 1 pt Marshmallow Root**
- 1 pt White Oak Bark
- ½ pt Black Sugar
- ½ pt Pumice

Use in magics intended to bring harmony, to help people get along who might not otherwise do so, or to create a generally peaceful, calm environment.

Sprinkle across doorways or in the corners of a room to end arguments, reduce hurt feelings, and to help encourage bickering or adversarial parties to get along. This powder can also be included in any spellwork intended to achieve the same results at a distance. It works particularly well when added to charms made from paper, small bottles, or ornaments which are then placed in the target space as decorations.

Black sugar may be obtained from some shops that sell baking decorations, particularly around the Halloween season. If it is not available in your area, regular white sugar mixed with charcoal may be substituted.

Persuasion Powder

To assist with eloquence and verbal persuasion.

Ingredients:

- 2 pt Marshmallow Root**
- 1 pt Galangal Root
- 1 pt Cherry Bark
- 1 pt Orris Root
- ½ pt Ground Allspice
- ½ pt Ground Cloves

(Black Sugar may be substituted for Marshmallow Root if it is more readily available.)

Use in magics intended to make your words ring true with your listeners, to sway them to your point of view without directly commanding, or to make your arguments strong and get your point across in a convincing fashion. Sprinkle a little pinch in your shoes before going to important meetings or interviews, or any time you feel like you might need your words to have a little extra punch.

Copal Resin may be added to this mix to create an incense. If you plan to do so, do not use sugar in the mix, as burning it may damage the vessel or leave a sticky, hard-to-clean residue.

Note: As tempting as it may seem, do not put this powder in your mouth as a method of application. If you want to sweeten your speech with magic using an edible focus, use sugar or a drop of honey, not Persuasion Powder.

Pet Protection Powder

For the protection and well-being of domestic animals

Ingredients:

- 2 pt Red Clover Blossoms & Leaves
- 1 pt White Oak Bark
- 1 pt Hyssop
- 1 pt Sweet Basil

For Cats – 1 pt Catnip
For Dogs – 1 pt Fennel
For Livestock – 1 pt Oats or Oatstraw
For Small Mammals – 1 pt Parsley
For Reptiles – 1 pt Nettle
For Fish or Amphibians – 1 pt Irish Moss (Carrageen)

Use in magics intended to protect the life and well-being of a pet or domestic animal. Bind a few pinches of the powder into a sachet or packet with an image of the animal which is to be protected. If shed fur, claws, scales, etc. are available, include these as well.

Please note that the use of this powder does not guarantee perfect health, complete prevention of accidents, or abnormally long life. It can only help to protect and succor the animal for the natural span of its' life. Be sure to employ good methods of mundane care and regular checkups to ensure good health.

*Do not use this powder topically on your pet. Do not put it in their food or water or in their enclosures. This powder is for non-contact magical use **only**.*

Pixie Dust

For augmentation of wish magic.

Ingredients:

- 2 pt Confectioner's Sugar
- 1 pt Rainbow or Gold Glitter
- ½ pt Powdered Violets
- ½ pt Powdered Dandelion Seeds

Use in magics that accompany the making of wishes. This powder was inspired by all the childhood rituals I've ever heard of that are supposed to make wishes come true, from puffing dandelion seeds to blowing out candles to calling dibs on the first stars to appear in the evening sky.

Place a small amount of Pixie Dust in the palm of the dominant hand and blow it out a window or to toss it onto a passing breeze help a wish come true. Carry a few pinches in small packet or vial to help long-term wishes come to fruition.

Note: Don't worry about making large amounts of Pixie Dust. A little of this goes a very long way!

Promisekeeper Powder

To seal vows and promises in spellwork.

Ingredients:

- 2 pt Rose Petals
- 1 pt Thyme
- 1 pt Scullcap**
- 1 pt Lavender
- ½ pt Strawflower
- ½ pt Cherry Blossom

Use in magics intended to seal a vow, to help keep a vow once made, or to remind someone of their promises. Include the powder in charms and spellcasting related to promises, vows, and bonds.

If the simple childhood spit shake to seal a promise is not for you, you might mix a pinch or two of the powder into some modeling clay. Form the clay into beads which each person involved in the vow will keep as a reminder.

If you're concerned that a promise made to you is in danger of being broken, put a pinch on a piece of paper with the subject's name, twist it into a packet, and burn it to remind them of their given word.

Prosperity Salt

For all-purpose prosperity, wealth-drawing, and money-related magics.

Ingredients:

- 3 pt Salt
- 1 pt Chamomile
- 1 pt Bergamot
- 1 pt Ginger Root
- 1 pt Spearmint
- ½ pt Juniper Berries
- ½ pt Bay Leaves

As with other prosperity and money-drawing substances, Prosperity Salt may be kept with a jar of seed money to draw wealth to the household. Since the recipe contains salt, it would be wise to keep the powder in a paper packet or a small bottle to prevent tarnish or corrosion to your coins over time.

A bottle of Prosperity Salt kept on the altar can help to draw wealth into the household. A small ornament can be made for the same purpose. Add pinches of the associated herbs in their whole form for visual interest.

I find Prosperity Salt to work best when seeking long-term prosperity and steady, sustainable income. If you're seeking fast money or short-term help, I'd suggest adding a bit of Catalyst Powder to the mix or trying Jackpot Powder instead.

Protection Powder

For general protection magic of all kinds.

Ingredients:

- 2 pt White Oak Bark
- 2 pt Green Sage
- 2 pt Basil (any kind)
- 1 pt White Willow Bark
- 1 pt Juniper
- 1 pt Hyssop
- 1 pt Vervain
- 1 pt Witch Hazel**
- ½ pt White Sage
- ½ pt Heather Blossom
- ½ pt Bloodroot**
- ½ pt Yarrow**
- ½ pt Solomon's Seal Root

Use in magics intended to provide strong protection for any object, dwelling, or living being. Combine with a resin base or your favorite incense powder to create burnable protection incense. This particular powder makes an excellent blend for censing associated with household wards and the casting of property protection spells.

If you regularly make ornament charms or witch webs for protection, this is a good default powder to include in their creation. It can also be added to paper charms or clay charms if you'd prefer something you can carry with you. I don't recommend wax charms for carry-along talismans, as they tend to deform or break apart easily.

This blend is all-purpose. There are a lot of ingredients, but it adds up to an extremely effective powder that covers all the most important bases. If you're wondering if a particular thing that you need protection against is included under that umbrella, the answer is most likely yes.

Purification Salt

For removing spells from enchanted items.

Ingredients:

- 3 pt Salt
- 1 pt Lavender
- 1 pt Vetiver
- 1 pt Lemon Verbena
- 1 pt Rosemary

Use for the removal of spells and magical effects from physical objects, including poppets, charms, spell jars, and ward anchors.

To purify an enchanted item, place the object into a container, cover it with Purification Salt, and let it sit overnight. Retrieve the item the next day. Discard the used salt after three uses. If you use and recycle objects for magical purposes on a frequent basis, this is a salt you may want to make in bulk.

Before burying the enchanted item, make sure that contact with the salt won't cause damage to the object. The concern is largely for items of jewelry which may tarnish during the process. A single day's burial in salt is not usually enough to cause noticeable damage, but I do recommend immediately rinsing and properly cleaning any jewelry immediately upon removal from the salt bin.

For practical purposes, make sure that you thoroughly clean and sanitize your spell jars before placing them in the salt. Some spell jars may contain rotten or moldy materials, or may carry bad smells if they've been sealed up for a while. Purification Salt only purifies magical residue; it can't really do anything for putrid leftovers.

Quick Draw Powder

For on-the-go activation of dormant spells and wards, or for quick defense.

Ingredients:

- 2 pt Salt
- 1 pt Cinnamon
- 1 pt Black Pepper
- 1 pt Cayenne
- 1 pt Ginger
- ½ pt Powdered Glass

Sometimes we leave home without protective charms or without activating personal protection spells. Quick Draw Powder is an on-the-go option which creates instant protection when you need it. No ritual or incantation required.

Put a pinch in your shoe or the footwells of your vehicle for a fast and easy protection spell, or toss it over your shoulder when leaving to prevent undesirables from following you home. Cast a palmful over your tracks to confuse and deter pursuers. If your personal protections are not constantly up when away from home, throw a pinch of powder on the ground and step on it to create a temporary protection spell until you get back.

The powdered glass can come from any type of scrap or craft glass you happen to find. For stronger results, you may want to use mirror glass. Put the glass pieces inside a plastic bag for freezer storage and grind them down with a mallet or heavy jar.

I don't recommend the use of a small mortar and pestle for grinding glass, as shards tend to jump out and pose a safety risk. Only use this method if you have a mortar that's at least two inches deep, with a heavy pestle to match, and even then, work slowly and carefully, or use the bag method.

Do not grind glass in a spice grinder.

Rest In Peace Powder

For gently laying non-adversarial spirits to rest.

Ingredients:

- 2 pt Willow Bark
- 1 pt Witch Hazel**
- 1 pt Vetiver
- 1 pt Basil
- ½ pt Boneset
- ½ pt Angelica Root

Use for spirit-laying when the spirit is a loved one or of some other mortal being of amiable nature, or for funerary rites for the beloved dead.

Rest In Peace Powder is generally most effective when applied to the corners of a house or property, or when added to a burning bowl for censing purposes. Frankincense or Myrrh resin may be added to create incense for funerals and life celebration ceremonies, or for rites of remembrance conducted on anniversaries or certain holidays.

The effect of Rest In Peace Powder is much gentler in its' effect than Banishing Powder, Ghost-Be-Gone Powder, or Spirit Salt. Rather than a firm, no-nonsense, "Get the hell out of my house," it's more of a polite, "Let's say goodbye now, it's time for you to leave." If you need something stronger than a cordial farewell or if the spirit in question is not a friendly one, use one of the alternative powders listed above.

Rose Salt

For removing harmful influences from relationships.

Ingredients:

- 3 pt Salt
- 1 pt Red Rose Petals
- 1 pt Pink Rose Petals
- 1 pt White Rose Petals

Note: Red, pink, and white are the colors that I find easiest to obtain, but if you have other preferences or other colors are easier for you to lay hands on, use them. If you cannot find three different colors of roses, use equal parts salt and rose petals in the color you are able to find.

Whether it's an overbearing in-law, a jealous friend, or a pushy coworker, we've all experienced the irritation of meddlers and the discouraging results of their intrusive ways. This powder can be used to remove or negate harmful outside influences from your relationships with others.

This salt is ideal for bottle charms and strewing, as well as sympathetic magic. Burying a poppet made to represent the harmful person in a container of Rose Salt for three days and three nights is a nice no-muss-no-fuss way to rid yourself of problematic influences.

Another method that I've found particularly effective for removing harmful influences is a candle binding. Carve a diamond weave or spiraling pattern around a taper candle, then rub the candle down with Rose Salt (or other relevant powder) until the grooves are filled in. If the powder does not adhere, use a cotton swab to lightly coat the grooves with cooking oil to help the powder stick. Burn down the candle to remove the harmful influence and discard any melted wax with your garbage.

To remove these influences effectively, be sure to exercise mundane methods such as putting your foot down, shutting down hurtful or abusive behavior, and maintaining open and honest communication with your near-and-dear.

Sealing Salt

For creating and sealing circles for ritual work.

Ingredients:

- 3 pt Salt
- 1 pt Angelica Root
- 1 pt Basil
- 1 pt Sage
- ½ pt Black Pepper

This salt is specially formulated for strengthening magic circles and containment figures. Use it to create strong boundaries for your working space.

As long as your intent is clear when casting your circle, a thin line of the salt will do. There's no need for large heaping piles, which will only be difficult to clean up when you're finished. Sealing Salt can also be used to outline sigils and symbols within your working space if needed.

Note: If you are doing your ritual work outside on bare ground or grass, do not use Sealing Salt for your circle, as it poses a threat to vegetation and soil quality.

Show-Me Salt

For general revelatory, divinatory, and truth-finding magics.

Ingredients:

- 3 pt Salt
- 2 pt Tea Leaves
- 1 pt Borage
- 1 pt Hibiscus Flower
- 1 pt Willow Bark

Use to augment your practices which deal with divination or truth-seeking. This includes work with tarot, oracle cards, pendulums, scrying, tasseography, or whatever your preferred method may be.

When performing divination, many practitioners will set up a workspace for their tools and devices. A small bottle or dish of Show-Me Salt can be placed in this space to add clarity and ease to your reading. It does not necessarily make the reading more accurate, but it may make it easier for you to interpret the results.

Items such as pendulums or card decks may be lightly dusted with the salt before use to enhance the subsequent working. Be careful not to use the salt on anything that would be damaged by the application, and do not allow items to sit in the salt.

Sickroom Salt

To aid in recovery from illness.

Ingredients:

- 3 pt Salt
- 1 pt Charcoal
- 1 pt Hyssop
- 1 pt Parsley
- ½ pt White Willow Bark

Use in magics intended to help someone heal from illness. This salt is largely meant for infectious diseases and may or may not be equally effective for chronically-manifesting illnesses.

To assist with recovery from illness, place a small bowl of Sickroom Salt in the room where the patient is convalescing. Even something as small as a shot glass will do. Change the salt daily or weekly, depending on the severity of the illness, until the patient is well again. Be sure to accompany this with all applicable practical medical measures.

For healing work at a distance, create a cloth or clay poppet named for or containing a strand of hair from the person in need of healing. Place the poppet atop a small dish of Sickroom Salt and place it in the sunlight for a full day. Afterward, put the dish where it won't be disturbed and wait one week. If the patient does not recover within seven days, change the salt and recast the spell. (Hopefully, someone will have taken the patient to see a doctor in the interim.)

Note: Keep in mind when using Sickroom Salt that healing magic is meant to augment, not replace, modern medicine. Spells for healing may work alongside mundane treatments, but should never be considered equivalent to or more effective than practical medical care.

Simple Joys Powder

To augment and amplify the good things in your life during times of difficulty or sorrow.

Ingredients:

- 1 pt Cocoa Powder
- 1 pt Rose Petals
- 1 pt Cherry Blossoms
- ½ pt Catnip
- ½ pt Lavender
- ½ pt Marjoram

Use this powder in spells for long-term emotional healing, where the subject is finding it difficult to recognize blessings or benefits in their life. This is helpful for recovering from heartbreak or loss, or a long streak of bad luck.

For relief of heartache from lost or unrequited love, draw a heart on a piece of paper and write your full name inside it. Make a paste by adding a few drops of water or your own tears to a pinch or two of Simple Joys Powder. Smear the paste on the paper to fill in the heart shape, then fold up the paper and leave it in a dish on a shelf to dry. Once the moisture has evaporated, burn the packet in your cauldron and scatter the ashes into the wind. (If burning is not an option, open the packet and scatter the dried powder from your bedroom window.)

For relief of heartache born of grief or sorrow or frustration, whisper your pains to a palmful of the powder. Cry if you need to. Then go outside and toss the powder over your left shoulder. If the wind is blowing, make sure you toss the powder so that it doesn't blow back on you.

For best results, this spellwork should be done alongside practical self-care and support methods, and should not be used to treat depression or other mood disorders. If you are struggling with such things, please seek outside assistance from friends, family, or a medical professional.

Spirit Salt

For edging conjuration circles and dispelling summoned entities.

Ingredients:

- 3 pt Salt
- 1 pt Angelica Root
- 1 pt Basil
- 1 pt Peppermint
- 1 pt White Willow Bark
- ½ pt Garlic
- ½ pt Clover Leaf
- ½ pt Cinquefoil

This salt is primarily for practitioners who engage in regular spirit work that deals with summoning circles and conjuration of human spirit entities. Stronger substances or additional talismans may be needed for higher-level spirit work, or summonings involving non-human entities. Use your best judgment and take all necessary precautions associated with this type of magic.

Use this salt to edge doorways and windowsills as well as summoning circles, similar to Banishing Powder. It may also be thrown into bonfires or burning bowls to end a ritual.

My experience with spirit work is largely limited to an annual dinner invitation to deceased friends and loved ones, and banishment of unwanted guests. I have found this salt to be effective with voluntarily-summoned human spirits and as a barrier against the wandering dead during liminal times. To assist further with laying spirits gently to their rest, see Rest In Peace Powder.

Note: If you choose to use Spirit Salt on a conjuration or summoning circle made out-of-doors, make sure that the salt does not fall on vegetation or bare ground, as it will cause harm to the health of the plants and soil.

Star Power Powder

For dispelling stage fright and performance anxiety.

Ingredients:

- 1 pt Agrimony**
- 1 pt Orris Root
- 1 pt Sweet Basil
- ½ pt Yarrow**
- ½ pt Fennel
- Pinch of fine-consistency Gold Glitter

Use in magic designed to help you maintain confidence and composure during public speaking or performance. Put a pinch in your shoes before theatrical performances or public speaking engagements, or carry a sealed bottle or paper packet of the powder for the same effect.

Another option is to dust a piece of jewelry or piece of clothing that you intend to wear with a few pinches of Star Power Powder, provided that the glitter will not have an adverse affect on the item in question.

If you are unable to do any of these things, create a paper-doll poppet of yourself, smear it with a thin layer of glue, and sprinkle it with a pinch or so of Star Power Powder. Give it a little high-five, and leave it somewhere safe at home before you leave for your performance.

Note: This powder may be of some small help with anxiety related to large social gatherings, but it is not a substitute for your regular coping methods or medicines.

STFU Powder

For any magic intended to shut someone up.

Ingredients:

- 1 pt Slippery Elm Bark
- 1 pt Deer's Tongue
- 1 pt Nettle Leaf
- ½ pt Sassafras
- ½ pt Bloodroot**

Use in magics intended to bind tongues, silence gossip, get people to stop speaking harshly to you, and make loud-mouthed jerks shut the hell up. Sprinkle where you know the target will be, particularly in meeting places where you know the target will be tempted to ramble on. Add to any spellwork intended to achieve the same effect at a distance.

If properly applied, this powder can also be used to rob someone of their eloquence, make them trip over their words, or say just the wrong thing at the worst possible time. One method of accomplishing this involves a jar and some fruit slices.

Slice a strawberry thinly lengthwise, then wrap one of the triangular slices in a slice of paper bearing the name of the target of the spell. Place the slice into a small jar, add a spoonful of STFU Powder, and cover with salt. The spell should last for the length of time that it takes for the strawberry slice to completely dry out.

Sweetening Powder

To change people's attitudes and actions towards you for the better.

Ingredients:

- 1 pt Sugar
- 1 pt Honeysuckle
- 1 pt Ginger
- ½ pt Orris Root
- ½ pt Cloves

Use in any spell where you need to increase the chances that someone will look on you in a positive light, especially where you need a decision to swing in your favor.

This powder is highly useful for attitude adjustments of all sorts. Add it to a paper charm or spell jar to improve the temperament of a grouchy or belligerent boss. Put a pinch in your shoes or carry a vial of the powder when going to ask for a raise. Dust your hands with it before discussing professional deals, bargaining with a realtor or car dealer, or going to court.

I've also found the attitude-improving properties of the powder to be very effective for uncomfortable family situations. It cannot change people's fundamental traits or beliefs, but when surreptitiously applied to the corners of one's sitting room, it may improve the dispositions of housemates and visitors. Persons inclined to be disagreeable may be more amiable, and persons inclined to be rude or passive-aggressive may be more polite.

The powder is also helpful, to a certain degree, for ending arguments and promoting more harmonious conversation, but this is a secondary effect. It's much more useful in matters of persuasion.

If necessary, this may be combined with Done Deal Powder for additional help in reaching beneficial financial agreements.

Threshold Powder

For barrier magic and protection of doorways and sacred spaces.

Ingredients:

- 2 pt Salt
- 1 pt Angelica Root
- 1 pt Peppermint
- 1 pt Elderflower
- 1 pt Rosemary
- ½ pt Cloves
- 1 crushed Cherry Pit per cup of powder

Please note that Cherry Pits (or Cherry Stones) may be difficult to crush or even break apart. The only reliable method I've found is to place the pit inside a sandwich bag and whack it repeatedly with a hammer. That's not even remotely exaggerated.

If for some reason you're unable to break up a Cherry Pit for your powder batch, you can store a clean, dry pit in the jar and use it as a blending ball to help keep the powder well-mixed.

Use the powder for heavy-duty barrier magic, where Banishing Powder or Black Salt have either failed or don't feel like the right option. The best method of deployment is to lay the powder across a threshold, as the name suggests, to protect a home or an individual room.

The powder can also be used to outline sacred spaces for ritual, spellcasting, or meditation. Be advised that if you are working with an outdoor space, you should *not* use this powder on grass, in a garden, or on bare dirt. The salt content will be harmful to the soil and the plant life. For outdoor barriers, you can replace the 2 parts Salt with dry soil from your yard, or with baking soda, which will not have the adverse effects of salt.

A simpler method, for those who can't be flinging handfuls of powders everywhere, is to hang a small bottle of Threshold Powder over your door or include it in the casting of protective barriers for your sacred spaces.

Traveler's Luck Powder

For protection from theft, accidents, and general ill fortune while traveling.

Ingredients:

- 2 pt Irish Moss (Carrageen)
- 2 pt White Oak Bark
- 1 pt Fenugreek
- 1 pt Feverfew
- ½ pt Black Cohosh**
- ½ pt Ground Nutmeg

Use in magics intended to keep oneself or other safe and free from mishaps on long trips or during frequent travel. Fold a few pinches into a paper packet containing your travel details. Tuck this into your luggage or glove compartment in your vehicle.

For more general travel protection, you can sprinkle a few pinches in the footwells of your car, or just keep a few blank paper packets or a bottle charm around if you frequently travel on short notice, or if you just want day-to-day protection.

Note: For readers familiar with the tangled web of inconvenience that is airport security, I recommend putting the packet of Traveler's Luck Powder into your checked luggage. If you're only taking a carry-on, use a single-ounce bottle (or smaller) and tuck it in with your toiletries. Hopefully these measures will help you avoid trouble. If you're going to be traveling in an area where security measures regarding luggage contents are extremely strict, put a tiny pinch inside your shoes, or create a protection charm that you can leave at home to work for your safe return.

Truthfinder Powder

Ingredients:

- 1 pt Copal Resin
- 1 pt Sugar

Use in magics intended to persuade someone to tell the truth, or to divine truth or hidden knowledge in confusing situations. Sprinkle the powder where you know the target will walk, be it on a doorstep or a walkway or what have you. You can specify a target or just let the magic work on its' own, in which case any person walking over it will feel inclined to tell the truth when put to the test or questioned directly.

This powder may also be used spellwork meant to encourage general honesty and truthfulness, or spells intended to help the caster determine truth from falsehood.

Note: This powder and its' effect are technically in the realm of compulsion magic. However, the effect is subtle and falls into a rather gray area in that regard.

Turning Salt

For counter magic and deflection.

Ingredients:

- 3 pt Salt
- 1 pt Vetiver
- 1 pt Agrimony**
- ½ pt Bloodroot**

Use in any magic intended to deflect, turn away, or directly oppose unwanted things, bad fortune, or the malicious magical efforts of another practitioner.

The best methods that I've found for using this powder deal with mirrors and poppets. You can create a mirror jar to deflect magical harm with a small mirror, a piece of paper describing the thing you're seeking to defend yourself against, and a few spoonfuls of Turning Salt. For more specific spells, a poppet named for the person sending magic against you may be filled with or buried in Turning Salt. Either method will send the effect back on the person who cast it. The poppet method is more effective simply because there's a name and a definite target involved, but the mirror spell works well for basic counter magic.

As I've mentioned before, it's very difficult to determine whether you're suffering the influence of baneful magic, or any magic you didn't create yourself, unless you physically sit there and watch someone cast it on you. And let's face it: few people who would want to sling hexes are that open about it, myself included. So if you suspect you've been hexed, I would recommend performing a cleansing or a hex removal spell before I'd suggest using counter magic. Save that for when you have some idea of where the trouble is coming from.

Weather Magic Powders

Please note before using any of these powders that weather magic can be tricky and should be undertaken with care. These powders are meant to be used sparingly. When in doubt, err on the side of caution. Always keep the natural weather patterns of your area in mind and remember that Less Is More.

Raincloud Powder
For the production of rain in weather spells
- 2 pt Ground Rice or Rice Flour
- 1 pt Salt
- 1 pt Bladderwrack or Ground Seaweed

Sunshine Powder
For reversing rain spells or bringing fair weather
- 1 pt Sunflower Petals
- 1 pt Goldenrod**
- 1 pt Calendula
- ½ pt Sugar or Honey Dust

Storm Salt
For calling up storms
- 2 pt Salt
- 1 pt Broom**
- 1 pt Bladderwrack
- ½ pt Birch Bark

Note: For best results, dissolve a spoonful of Storm Salt in a bowl of water and leave outdoors to evaporate.

Windraiser Powder
To call the winds
- 1 pt Dandelion Leaf
- 1 pt Dulse
- 1 pt Alder
- ½ pt Broom**

Wizard Blizzard Powder
For production of snow and ice
- 1 pt Confectioner's Sugar
- 1 pt Juniper or Pine Needles
- ½ pt Holly
- ½ pt Ivy

Clear Skies Powder
To create clear weather or negate previous weather magics
- 1 pt Solomon's Seal Root
- 1 pt Calendula Petals
- ½ pt Vetiver
- ½ pt Cloves

Note: If especial strength is needed to undo previous weather magics (i.e. if a storm has gotten out of control), add a few threads of Saffron to the blend.

Bree's Lunar Salt
For augmentation of moon-related magics
- 3 pt Salt
- 1 pt Jasmine
- 1 pt Willow Bark
- 1 pt Honeysuckle or White Rose Petals
- Few Drops of Lotus Scented Oil (if desired)

Bree's Solar Salt
For augmentation of sun-related magics
- 3 pt Salt
- 1 pt Calendula
- 1 pt Ginger Root
- 1 pt Goldenrod** or Dandelion Blossoms
- Few Drops of Lemon Verbena Essential Oil (if desired)

Section Two:

Magical Oils

Attraction, Love, & Glamour

Bachelor's Buttons Attraction Oil
To attract a companion
- Cornflower Blossoms
- Passionflower Herb**
- Pink Rose Petals

Belle of the Ball Beauty Oil
For beauty glamours
- Orange Peel
- Magnolia Petal
- Maidenhair Fern
- Primrose Blossoms**

Come On Baby Light My Fire Lust Oil
For increasing sexual attraction in consensual encounters
- Passionflower Herb**
- Savoury
- Ginger Root, Fresh
- Red Rose Petals

Note: Use Responsibly. Practice Safe Sex.

Happy Couple Preservation Oil
To preserve peace and harmony in a relationship
- Hibiscus Flowers
- Buttercups
- Orris Root
- Tea Tree Essential Oil

Look My Way Attraction Oil
To turn the head of a possible romantic partner
- Clover Blossoms
- Pink Rose Petals
- Lovage
- Apple or Tomato Seeds

(Note: This does not affect free will, it just gets their attention.)

Magnetic Me Attraction Oil
For attraction spells of all kinds
- Cinnamon Stick
- Cardamom**
- Bay Leaf
- Sassafras Leaf

Own the Runway Confidence Oil
For supreme confidence
- Yarrow**
- Sumac Berries
- Ginger Root, Fresh

Pass Unseen Stealth Oil
For perceived invisibility glamours
- Cherry Bark or Blossoms
- Poppy Seeds**
- Devil's Shoestring**
- Dogwood Blossoms (if available)

Sugar-Me Attraction Oil
To attract a wealthy benefactor
- Honeysuckle
- Clover Blossoms
- Peppermint
- Tea Leaves

Augmentation

Blazing Shield Resilience Oil
To recover strength and robustness
- Carnation
- Cinquefoil
- Fennel
- Pine Needles

Cauldronkeeper Wisdom Oil
To enhance intuition and wisdom
- Hazel
- Elder
- Sage
- Peach Pit (in master bottle)

Clear the Fog Concentration Oil
To boost concentration and focus
- Bay Leaf
- Peppermint
- Vanilla Bean
- Tea Tree Essential Oil

Note: Does not treat attention or focus disorders.

Fresh Eyes Inspiration Oil
For new perspective and fresh inspiration on difficult projects
- Peppermint
- Horehound
- Patchouli

Full Moon Lunar Affinity Oil
For augmentation of spells attuned to the lunar cycle
- Willow Bark
- Jasmine Flowers
- Fennel
- Mugwort**

Note: Use With Caution.

Get Me Through the Day Endurance Oil
For a tiny extra boost on those low-energy days
- Lemon Verbena
- White Oak Bark
- Rosemary
- Echinacea**

High Noon Solar Affinity Oil
For augmentation of spells attuned to the solar cycle
- Calendula Petals
- Chamomile
- Bay Leaf
- Eyebright

Note: Use With Caution.

Honeytongue Eloquence Oil
For verbal persuasion and effective speech
- Honeysuckle
- Orris Root
- Licorice Root
- Marshmallow Root**

Note: Do not consume.

Increase the Thing Empowerment Oil
For self-empowerment and glamours pertaining thereto
- Petunia Petals
- Bergamot
- Lemon Verbena
- Sunflower Petals

Jack-of-all-Trades Work Enhancement Oil
For augmentation of workplace abilities
- Sweet Basil
- Meadowsweet**
- Borage Flowers
- Vanilla Bean

Lionheart Courage Oil
For bravery and confidence spells
- Black Tea Leaves
- Bay Leaf
- Cedar Tips
- Thyme Sprigs

Magical Me Power Boost Oil
For augmentation of spellcasting
- Ginger Root
- Rosemary
- Bergamot
- Cedar Tips

No Fear Here Bravery Oil
To reduce fear and anxiety in worrisome situations
- Yarrow**
- Nettle Leaf
- Tea Leaves
- Orange or Neroli Essential Oil

Note: Does not treat anxiety-related disorders.

Seer's Supplement Scrying Oil
For anointing divination tools
- Periwinkle**
- Caraway Seeds
- Lemon Balm
- Mugwort**

Note: Use With Caution.

Shrink-Me Reduction Oil
For augmentation of weight loss spells
- Chives or Green Onions
- Fennel
- Dill
- Bergamot

Note: Use alongside mundane healthy weight loss measures. Do not use if you have an eating disorder.

Stargazer Wishing Oil
For augmentation of wish magic
- Violets
- Spearmint
- Willow Bark
- Dandelion Blossoms

Steel Backbone Fortitude Oil
For bravery and endurance
- Blue Vervain
- Pine Needles
- Cedar Tips
- Yarrow**

Study Buddy Memory Oil
For retaining what you've studied
- Rosemary
- Bergamot
- Caraway Seeds

Third Thoughts Intuition Oil
For enhancement of instinctive intelligence
- Oak Bark
- Sunflower Petals
- Witch Hazel**
- Cedar Tips

Watchful Eye Viewing Oil
To enhance powers of observation
- Grape Leaf
- Lemon Balm
- Rosemary
- Celery Seed (or dried leaf from stalks)

Note: Do not apply to skin around eyes. Do not apply directly to eyeballs either.

Catalysts & Change

1000% Done Resolution Oil
For resolution of arguments, conflicts, and general drama
- Mullein Leaf
- Nettle Leaf
- Rosemary

Brand New Me Transformation Oil
For self-improvement, physical changes, or personal growth
- Fennel
- Lady's Mantle**
- Pine Needles
- Geranium Essential Oil

Note: If your personal journey includes adjusting to a change in gender or sexuality, add a few Persimmon seeds to the mix.

Hard Restart Changebringer Oil
To bring significant change or action in a stagnant situation
- Ginger Root
- Fennel
- Anise

Note: Use With Caution

Jump-Start Catalyst Oil
To give events in motion a "jump" to move things along
- Bergamot
- Peppermint
- Cinnamon Stick

Period of Adjustment Oil
To assist with adapting to unexpected life changes
- Lady's Mantle**
- Fennel
- Parsley
- Peppermint

Posthaste Catalyst Oil
For when it absolutely, positively has to happen on-schedule
- Bergamot
- Cardamom**
- Ginger Root
- Sandalwood or Amber Oil

Putting Down Roots Stability Oil
For adjusting to a new home or situation
- Licorice Root
- Fennel
- Star Anise Seeds
- Apple Seeds

Six Impossible Things Oil
To help oneself obtain or maintain a positive attitude
- Basil
- Marjoram
- Rosemary
- Borage Flower

Cleansing & Banishing

Banned From The Premises Banishing Oil
For anointing doorways and banishing unwanted persons
- Oregano
- Rosemary
- Lemon Peel
- Thyme

Clear the Air Cleansing Oil
For cleansing after arguments, grief, or general negativity
- Marjoram
- Dandelion Leaf
- Wintergreen**

Feed the Void Banishing Oil
For banishing things that need to vanish...permanently
- Solomon's Seal Root
- Feverfew
- Boneset
- Mandrake* **

First Do No Harm Cleansing Oil
For getting rid of harmful influences and persons
- Sassafras Leaf
- Bay Leaf
- Eucalyptus**
- Rosemary

Fresh Start Cleansing Oil
For cleansing and renewal spells
- Rosemary
- Peppermint
- Lavender
- Lemon Peel

Get Gone Banishing Oil
For banishing spells of all kinds
- Sweet Basil
- Cloves
- Vetiver

Note: Safe for candle dressing.

Hot Foot Banishing Oil
For banishing spells of all kinds
- Chili Peppers
- Cumin
- Black Peppercorns

Note: Do not use for candle dressing, as the volatile oils from the chili peppers may be harmful if inhaled in aerosol form.

No Means No Repulsion Oil
For repelling obnoxiously persistent suitors
- Horseradish
- Lemon Peel
- Lime Peel
- Blue Vervain

Not In My House Banishing Oil
For clearing a home of unwelcome, unruly persons or entities
- Fleabane
- Nettle Leaf
- Black Peppercorns
- Cloves
- Steel Pin or Sewing Needle in master bottle

Note: If meant for the living, apply to the soles of their shoes. If meant for metaphysical beings or for general use, apply over the lintel of the front door with middle finger of dominant hand.

Healing & Restoration

Brim With Vim Vitality Oil
To restore flagging magical energy and clear post-spell haze
- Tangerine (Satsuma) Peel
- Cinnamon Stick
- Ginger Root
- Vervain

Catch Some Z's Restful Sleep Oil
For restful sleep spells and dream magic
- Lavender Flowers
- Spearmint Leaves
- Vanilla Bean

Clear Head Confusion Dispeller Oil
To help dispel mental funk and promote clarity of thought
- Basil
- Bay Leaf
- Lemon Peel
- Tea Tree Essential Oil

Flu Season Sickness Repelling Oil
For preventing illness alongside mundane medicine
- Orange Peel
- Lemon Peel
- Ginger Root
- Echinacea**

Free to Fly Bondbreaker Oil
For severing attachments and bindings
- Horseradish Root
- Sassafras Leaf
- Sumac Berries
- Vetiver

Get-Well-Soon Healing Oil
For augmentation of healing and recovery spells
- Thyme Sprigs
- Juniper Berries
- Peppermint
- Wintergreen**

Gimme Closure Recovery Oil
For recuperation and closure after heartbreak or grief
- Hyacinth
- Lavender
- Marjoram
- Witch Hazel**

Note: For deep emotional pain, a single Balm of Gilead bud may be added to the master bottle. (These may be difficult to find.)

Simple Dispelling Oil
For general all-purpose removal of magical effects
- Angelica Root
- Blue Vervain
- Lemon Peel

Note: For best results, rub the oil onto a fresh egg, pass the egg over the person or object seven times, and discard the egg.

Sleep Sweet Dreampillow Oil
For the anointing of bedside sachets and dream pillows
- Lavender
- Eucalyptus**
- Spearmint
- Vanilla

Note: Does not treat insomnia. Do not use if allergic.

Soothe-Me Stress Reducer Oil
For reducing stress and anxiety
- Bayberry Essential Oil
- Passionflower Herb**
- Lemon Balm

Note: Does not treat anxiety or mood disorders.

Sore No More Healing Oil
For assistance in spells focused on relieving physical pain
- Willow Bark
- Wintergreen**
- Juniper Berries
- Rosemary Sprigs

Note: Not for medical use.

Temperance Habit-Breaker Oil
For magics intended to help one break bad habits
- Dried Minced Onion
- Borage Flowers
- Lemon Grass

Witchcraft and Chill Calmative Oil
To calm the mind before spellcasting or ritual work
- Meadowsweet**
- Lemon Balm
- Lavender
- Witch Hazel**

Hexing & Hexbreaking

All-Purpose Hexing Oil
For general hexing, cursing, and baneful magic
- Dried Chili Pepper
- Lime Peel
- Lemongrass
- Rusted Nail in master bottle

All-Purpose Hexbreaking Oil
For general negation of baneful spells cast by oneself or others
- Agrimony**
- Cinquefoil
- Fennel
- Vervain
- Solomon's Seal Root in master bottle

Backhanded Blessing Oil
For blessings that are anything but benevolent
- Burnt Cinquefoil
- Bay Leaf
- Pine Needles
- Bayberry Root

Blue Moon Curse Reversal Oil
For turning and countering baneful magic
- Angelica Root
- Lemon Verbena
- Motherwort**
- Elderberries*

Eye of Newt Disruption Oil
For disrupting and confounding magical efforts against you
- Black Mustard Seeds
- Bloodroot**
- Nettle Leaf
- Garlic (1 clove, bruised)

Golden Apple Discord Oil
To sow dissent and cause arguments
- Apple Seeds (preferably from a yellow apple)
- Peony Seeds*
- Tormentil Root
- Chicory Root

No Rest For The Wicked Hexing Oil
For punishing one's enemies
- Chili Pepper (any)
- Horseradish Root
- Cramp Bark
- Bayberry Root

No Strings On Me Uncrossing Oil
For nullifying hexes or harmful influences on oneself
- Chamomile
- Sassafras Leaf
- Lemon Verbena
- Slice of Fresh Ginger Root

On Your Own Head Retribution Oil
For counter magic and revenge hexes
- Elderberries*
- Bloodroot**
- Devil's Shoestring**
- Vetiver

Reversal of Fortune Bad Luck Oil
For turning good luck into bad
- Blueberry Leaves or Bark
- Lemongrass
- Lemon Seeds or Peel
- Lime Peel or Essential Oil

Wicked Witch Heavy-Duty Cursing Oil
For occasions when a regular-strength hex just won't do
- Wormwood* **
- Ghost Chili Pepper
- Lemon Seeds
- Lobelia*

Note: Use With Extreme Caution.

Luck, Money, & Success

Bestseller Business Enhancement Oil
To attract sales and business revenue
- Orange Peel
- Willow Bark
- Marjoram
- Parsley

Blue Shell Success Oil
To achieve success by removing competition
- Blue Violets
- Bay Leaf
- Woodruff
- Galangal Root

Clear the Way Obstacle Remover Oil
For overcoming difficulty and attracting new opportunities
- Dried Sumac Berries
- Ginger Root
- Sweet Basil

Golden Fields Prosperity Oil
For abundance, good fortune, and general well-being
- Sesame or Pumpkin Seeds
- Wheat or Barley Kernels
- Orange Peel
- Honeysuckle

Green Light Fast Luck Oil
For swift improvement of personal fortunes
- Spearmint
- Bergamot
- Marjoram
- Patchouli

Make A Wish Oil
For wish-making spells of all kinds
- Spearmint Leaves
- Lemon Balm
- Bay Leaf
- Violet Blossoms

Moneybags Cashbringer Oil
To bring a quick monetary boost when you need it
- Goldenseal Root (sub. Oregon Grape Root**)
- Ginger Root
- Goldenrod**
- Allspice Berries

My Day in Court Justice Oil
For victory in legal matters
- Calendula Petals
- Honeysuckle
- Galangal Root
- Sumac Berries

Retirement Fund Wealth Oil
For long-term financial gains with reliable footing
- Orange Essential Oil
- Straw Flower*
- Chamomile
- Oak Bark
- Saffron (single thread in master bottle)

Note: This will not pay off in the short-term, so use it only for money spells that aren't associated with an immediate need.

Rich Witch Money-Draw Oil
For wealth and prosperity spells
- Orange Peel
- Dried Allspice Berries
- Marjoram Sprigs

Roundabout Luck-Turning Oil
For turning bad luck into good
- Ginger Root
- Peppermint Leaves
- Orange Peel
- Thyme Sprigs

What I'm Owed Debt Repayment Oil
For collecting on outstanding debts that are owed to you
- Bayberry Root or Essential Oil
- Bergamot
- Yarrow**

Winner's Circle Success Oil
For success spells of all kinds
- Bergamot
- Ginger Root
- Cloves
- Lemon Balm

Wolves At The Door Debt-Dodger Oil
For a brief reprieve from collectors while your finances improve
- Dogbane Leaf
- Sumac Berries
- Bayberry Root
- Peppermint or Pennyroyal**

Persuasion & Manipulation

Dance Puppet Dance Command Oil
To influence others to follow instructions or see things your way
- Galangal Root
- Marshmallow Root**
- Sassafras Leaf
- Bloodroot**

Note: Use With Caution.

Final Rebuttal Argument-Ender Oil
For resolving disagreements in decisive fashion
- Rosemary
- Passionflower Herb**
- Valerian**
- Yarrow**

Gimme Some Sugar Persuasion Oil
For persuasion spells of all kinds
- Lemon Verbena
- Honeysuckle
- Marshmallow Root**

It Wasn't Me Diversion Oil
For diverting suspicion from yourself or your actions
- Dogbane
- Cherry Bark
- Blueberry Leaves
- Marshmallow Root**

Loyal to the End Fidelity Oil
To encourage faithful devotion and strong allegiance
- Raspberry Leaf**
- Licorice Root
- Thyme Sprigs
- Cardamom**

Mysterious Me Secrecy Oil
For maintaining confidences and keeping your secrets hidden
- Juniper Berries
- Raspberry Leaves
- Poppy Seeds**
- Licorice Root

Note: Works best when fewer individuals are involved.

Palm of My Hand Command Oil
To take strong control of a situation
- Galangal Root
- Sassafras Root
- Cardamom**
- Tobacco

Note: Use With Caution.

Pull Your Weight Oil
For slacking coworkers or lazy housemates
- Galangal Root
- Sumac Berries
- Orris Root
- Cinnamon

Red-Hot Poker Command Oil
For control of any situation
- Cinnamon Stick (in master bottle)
- Ginger Root (fresh)
- Galangal Root
- Tobacco

Secretkeeper Oil
To bind sworn oaths and prevent loose lips
- Juniper Berries
- Pine Needles
- Clover Leaves

Sweet Nothings Persuasion Oil
To assist with verbal persuasion magics.
- Stevia Leaf
- Strawberry Slice
- Honeysuckle
- Marshmallow Root**

Truth Be Told Honesty Oil
To encourage people to tell the truth
- Cherry Blossoms
- Borage Flowers
- Tea Leaves
- Violets

Protection & Blessing

All-Purpose Blessing Oil
For blessing, purification, and consecration
- Lavender
- Sweet Basil
- Bay Leaf
- Patchouli

Note: Use Olive Oil for the base.

And Stay Out Ward Refresher Oil
For strengthening household protections between castings
- Sarsaparilla
- Oakmoss
- Horehound
- Sweet Basil

A Thousand Welcomes Blessing Oil
For a small blessing upon visitors to your home
- Meadowsweet**
- Pink Roses
- Bay Leaf
- Parsley

Change the Locks Protection Oil
For protection of the home from banished persons
- Cumin
- Oregano
- Rosemary
- Thistle

Cradlekeeper Child Protection Oil
For protection of infants and young children
- Daisies (any color)
- Flax Seeds
- Caraway Seeds
- Lamb's Ear Leaf

Note: Use to anoint the lintel of the door to the child's room.

Hearthside Home Blessing Oil
For a comfortable and harmonious home
- Sweet Basil
- Vervain
- Pine Needles
- Willow Bark

No More Monsters Bedroom Guardian Oil
For keeping scary things out of children's bedroom
- Witch Hazel**
- Elecampane
- Peppermint

Note: Makes good Monster Spray. Works for grown-up kids too!

No Soliciting Front Door Oil
To keep unwanted visitors away from your home
- Ivy Leaves
- Sweet Basil
- Blueberry Leaf
- Juniper Berries

Safe Space Protection Oil
To help one find sanctuary when it is most needed
- Blackberry Leaf (or Tea)
- Allspice Berries
- Fennel Tops
- Clover Leaves and Blossoms

The Shielding Light Protection Oil
For passive protective magics
- Caraway Seeds
- Eucalyptus Leaf**
- Lavender
- Vervain

Note: Passive protection magic functions as a shield, rebuffing or neutralizing harm. It is good for long-term spells that don't require much energy or maintenance.

The Shining Dark Protection Oil
For active protective magics
- Coconut Husk
- Thistle Leaf
- Witch Hazel**
- Angelica Root

Note: Active protection magic functions as a sword, strongly deflecting or fending off harm. This is best for short-term or immediate-use spells that are not meant to last, but must kick in very strongly and very quickly. Excellent for emergency personal protections.

The Sorcerer's Tower Protection Oil
To protect your witchy supplies and workspace from interlopers
- Juniper Sprigs or Berries
- Blueberry Leaf
- Thistle
- Astragalus Root

Note: Works best alongside mundane secrecy and privacy measures. To avoid damage, anoint containers, furniture, and doors rather than items. Do not use directly on books as it may damage delicate paper or covers. Use with caution on unfinished wood.

Thorn in the Door Warding Oil
To discourage unfriendly witches from entering your home
- Rosemary
- Bay Leaf
- Sage (any color)
- Solomon's Seal Root
- Rose Stem (with thorns) in master bottle

Walking Ward Protection Oil
For personal warding spells of all kinds
- Sweet Basil
- Witch Hazel**
- Fennel Sprigs

Note: This works for both active and passive protection magics and may be used in conjunction other protective oils.

Wanderlust Traveling Oil
For all-purpose protection and luck while traveling
- Feverfew
- Cinquefoil
- Witch Hazel**
- Spearmint

Witchbane Warding Oil
For repelling and countering harmful spells
- Bay Leaves
- Elderflower
- Star Anise
- Birch Bark

Miscellaneous

All-Purpose Candle Dressing Oil
For all-purpose candle anointing
- Sweet Basil
- Hyssop
- Clover Blossoms

All-Purpose Offertory Oil
For anointing of altar candles or offering dishes
- Red Rose Petals
- Rosemary
- Star Anise Pods
- Hyssop

Brought to the Light Revelation Oil
For revelatory and truth-finding magics
- Deer's Tongue Herb
- Borage Flowers
- Dandelion Heads
- Primrose Flowers or Essential Oil**

Note: If pregnant or nursing, substitute Violets for Primrose.

Done in the Dark Concealment Oil
For secrecy, confidentiality, and general deception
- Juniper Berries
- Licorice Root
- Thyme
- Ferns or Dried Seaweed

Note: For the final ingredient, use whichever is easier to obtain. Both bracken and seaweed work well for basic concealment spells.

Dreamweaver Nocturnal Visions Oil
To increase the chances of lucid or prophetic dreams
- Tea Leaves
- Willow Bark
- Jasmine
- Lemon Balm

Just Peachy Positivity Oil
For contentment and general optimism
- Rose Petals (any color)
- Sweet Basil
- Lavender
- Catnip
- Peach Pit in master bottle

Object Enchantment Anointing Oil
For attaching spells to portable or wearable objects.
- Honeysuckle
- Cardamom**
- Bergamot
- Lemon Verbena

Sunshiney Day Happiness Oil
To bring happiness and contentment
- Orange Peel
- Rose Petals
- Sweet Basil

Note: Does not treat depression or mood disorders.

Tangled Shoelaces Binding Oil
To impede someone's ability to move or act against you
- Pine Needles
- Devil's Shoestring**
- Scullcap**
- Coffee Grounds
- Iron Nail in master bottle

Tearoom Forbearance Oil
For when you need to keep your temper...no matter what
- Tea Leaves
- Meadowsweet**
- Echinacea**
- Fir Balsam Essential Oil

Truthteller Divination Oil
For augmentation of divinatory practices
- Evening Primrose**
- Hibiscus Flowers
- Celery Seeds
- Tea Leaves

Veilthinner Conjuration Oil
For summoning and conjuration of spirits
- Acacia
- Elderberries*
- Lilac Blossoms
- Sweetgrass

Note: Use With Caution.

Waycloser Spirit-Laying Oil
For sending off conjured spirits or laying them to rest
- Angelica Root
- Bay Leaves
- Vetiver
- Willow Bark

Magical Powder Recipe

Name: _____

Purpose: _____
_____
_____

Ingredients & Proportions:
- _____
- _____
- _____
- _____
- _____
- _____
- _____
- _____

Notes & Suggested Uses:

Magical Oil Recipe

Name: _____

Purpose: _____
_____
_____

Ingredients:
- _____
- _____
- _____
- _____
- _____

Notes & Suggested Uses:

Happy Witching!

Online Resources

Ruth Roy's Wellcat Herbs
http://www.wellcat.com/herbs.html
A highly reputable seller with quality herbs, teas, incense, and botanicals. I've been visiting her shop for years and I've always gotten good quality product for very reasonable prices. The proprietor also runs a booth every year at the Pennsylvania Renaissance Faire.

Starwest Botanicals
http://www.starwest-botanicals.com/
Bulk botanicals supplier for herbs, spices, oils, and teas. Good amount of organic and Fair Trade products, as well as supplies for holistic medicine and tea-making. This is my go-to store for larger amounts of the herbs that I can't grow myself or purchase from Mistress Ruth, as well as bulk muslin bags for charms.

The Magickal Cat
http://www.themagickalcat.com/
Online shop with just about everything you could want for your craft, from herbs to books to cauldrons, and everything in between. Reliable shipping and excellent customer service. The Magickal Cat is the equivalent of having a small-town witch shop right there on your browser.

AzureGreen
http://www.azuregreen.net/
One of the oldest and largest pagan supply stores in the United States, AzureGreen carries nearly any sort of ritual tool or crafting implement you could want for your practice, as well as a wide assortment of jewelry, decorations, books, music, and pagan-themed gift items.

Mountain Rose Herbs
https://www.mountainroseherbs.com/
A quality purveyor of bulk organic herbs, spices, and sundries. The site also carries aromatherapy products and essential oils, and has links to schools that offer courses in herbalism and herbology. If you're interested in making your own candles or bath products, this is a good place to find supplies.

Candlewic

http://www.candlewic.com/

For witches looking to get into candlemaking, Candlewic is an excellent place to start. From wax pellets to color blocks to a library of scents, you can find just about everything you need to build your workshop. Candlewic also offers tips and advice for first-time candlemakers, as well as a number of how-to videos.

Save On Scents

http://saveonscents.com/

If you can't find the scent you want in Candlewic's library, chances are the Save On Scents will have it and three more in the same family, at wholesale prices. Curious or cautious buyers can order small sample tubes to test fragrances before purchasing full-sized bottles. And if you find something you particularly enjoy, Save On Scents carries a wide variety of incense in all the classic scents, plus hundreds more. (Fair warning: This site is very addictive!)

Specialty Bottle

http://www.specialtybottle.com/

Wholesale bottles, jars, and vials of just about every size you can imagine. Very low prices, although shipping can be a bear (glass jars are heavy and require a lot of packing material). Still an excellent source for bulk quantities of any glassware you might want for your craft.

Seed Savers Exchange

http://www.seedsavers.org/

Non-profit organization dedicated to saving and sharing heirloom seeds. Ideal for anyone wishing to find seeds for a witchy garden. If you want to grow your own White Sage, this is the place to get seeds.

BioDiverSeed

http://www.biodiverseed.com/

A seed-swap website devoted to the exchange of primarily self-harvested, organic, and heirloom seeds. A great place to find seeds for fruits, vegetables, herbs, and flowers, including some you might not find in a typical garden shop.

Bibliography & Recommended Reading

Magic and Witchcraft

Cunningham, Scott. *Encyclopedia of Magical Herbs*. Llewellyn Publications, 1988.

--------. *Magical Herbalism: The Secret Craft of the Wise*. Llewellyn Publications, 1982 and 1983.

--------. *The Complete Book of Incenses, Oils and Brews*. Llewellyn Publications, 2002 edition.

diGregorio, Sophia. *Traditional Witches' Formulary and Potion-making Guide: Recipes for Magical Oils, Powders and Other Potions*. Winter Tempest Books, 2012.

Dugan, Ellen. *Garden Witchery: Magick from the Ground Up*. Llewellyn Publications, 2003.

--------. *Garden Witch's Herbal: Green Magick, Herbalism, and Spirituality*. Llewellyn Publications, 2009.

Furie, Michael. *Supermarket Magic: Creating Spells, Brews, Potions & Powders From Everyday Ingredients*. Llewellyn Publications, 2013.

Heldstab, Celeste Rayne. *Llewellyn's Complete Formulary of Magical Oils*. Llewellyn Publications, 2012.

Illes, Judika. *Encyclopedia of 5,000 Spells*. HarperOne, 2009.

Morrison, Dorothy. *Utterly Wicked: Curses, Hexes, & Other Unsavory Notions*. WillowTree Press LLC, 2007.

Moura, Ann. *Grimoire for the Green Witch*. Llewellyn Publications, 2003.

Practical Herbology

Chevalier, Andrew (FNIMH). *Encyclopedia of Herbal Medicine, Second Edition*. DK Publishing, 2000.

-------. *Herbal Remedies*. Metro Books. 2010 Edition. (Originally published 2007, Dorling Kindersly Limited, London.)

Culpeper, Nicholas. *Culpeper's Complete Herbal and English Physician*. Magna Books, 1992 edition. (Orig. published 1826.)

Fetrow, Charles W. (Pharm.D.) and Avila, Juan R. (Pharm.D.) *The Complete Guide to Herbal Medicines*. Pocket Books, 2000.

Green, James. *The Herbal Medicine-Maker's Handbook: A Home Manual*. Crossing Press. 2000.

Griggs, Barbara. *The Green Witch Herbal: Restoring Nature's Magic in Home, Health & Beauty Care*. Healing Arts Press. 1994.

About the Author

Bree NicGarran grew up in the wilds of Bucks County, PA, and now resides outside of Colonial Williamsburg in Virginia. She started reading at an early age and began writing shortly thereafter. Bree has been a practitioner of cottage witchcraft for over ten years, and specializes in plant-based magics. When she's not creating new spells or mucking about in the garden, she finds time to delve into fiction as well, and her works of short horror have been featured on various podcasts.

Her first solo book, *Grovedaughter Witchery: Practical Spellcraft*, was published in January 2017. It has received rave reviews and is being hailed by the online pagan community as the new must-have book for beginner witches. Bree is currently hard at work on a second volume of fairy-tale spells, along with an anthology of short stories.

In addition to her writing, Bree maintains a blog about and answering questions pertaining to cottage witchery. She currently lives with her husband and two very spoiled ginger cats, and she is very glad that none of them seem to mind having a pagan altar in the living room.

Related Works

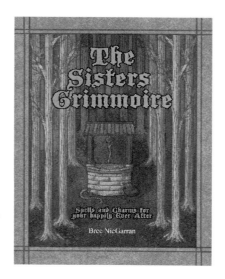

The Sisters Grimmoire:
Spells and Charms For Your Happily Ever After
(Second Edition)

Inspired by the well-known works of The Brothers Grimm, this volume boasts over sixty original spells lovingly crafted from favorite fairy tales, along with helpful spellcrafting instructions and several indices to aid you in your journey. All of this is wrapped up with useful chapter forewords discussing the various themes within the tales, some insight into the creative process, and a bit of discussion on ethics and the usage of magic.

Whether you're ready to yell "All Heads Off But Mine," looking to turn your luck around with some Buried Coins, or just wanting to show the world What Big Teeth you have, there is sure to be a spell within these pages that is exactly what you've been looking for.

After all, who couldn't use a bit of Happily Ever After?

Grovedaughter Witchery: Practical Spellcraft

For the witch whose town is devoid of occult shops and covens, learning the craft can be a daunting task indeed. Fortunately, there are plenty of ways for a budding practitioner to make a start

Discover the surprising ways you can practice your craft with commonplace items from the supermarket and the craft store. Build a travel kit for on-the-go magic. Create your own spells from scratch with a step-by-step guide. Learn how to make your own witch webs and magical powders. Uncover the secrets of walnut charms and witchballs and much, much more. Every page carries tricks of the trade and homegrown charms from the files of the Grovedaughter herself.

Available through Amazon in print and on Kindle e-readers.